GREENLAND

JD ROSSETTI

GREENLAND

CONTENTS

About the Author
258

Print ISBN: 979-8-9928656-2-2
Ebook ISBN: 979-8-9928656-3-9

FORWORD

What if the United States expanded beyond its current borders and Greenland became the 51st state? Sounds like a wild fantasy—or is it? In this witty yet deeply analytical exploration, Greenland: The 51st State? unpacks one of the most fascinating "what-if" scenarios in modern geopolitics.

Greenland, the world's largest island, has long been a land of icy mystery, Viking legends, and strategic military importance. But beneath the glaciers and the Northern Lights lies a deeper question: Could, or even should, Greenland become an American state? And what would that mean for both nations?

With a mix of historical insight, political analysis, and humor, this book delves into the serious and not-so-serious implications of Greenlandic statehood. From the U.S. military's past attempts to buy Greenland to the economic and cultural transformations that could follow statehood, this book covers every angle—the good, the bad, and the downright bizarre.

Inside These Pages, You'll Discover:
* The Hidden History of Greenland – From Norse explorers to Danish rule, how this icy land became a geopolitical hotspot.
* America's Love Affair with Greenland – Why the U.S. has tried (and failed) to buy Greenland multiple times.
* The Perks and Pitfalls of Statehood – Would Greenland thrive as part of the U.S., or lose its unique identity?

* Economic and Military Implications – From natural resources to Arctic dominance, why Greenland is more valuable than you think.

* Cultural Clashes and Conundrums – Could Greenlanders embrace American football, fast food, and federal bureaucracy?

* How Greenlandic Statehood Could Shift U.S. Elections – A new electoral battleground or just a political pipe dream?

* International Backlash – Would Denmark, China, or Russia have something to say about all this? (Spoiler: Yes, and it won't be pretty.)

* The Role of Climate Change – As Greenland's ice melts, could its future be reshaped by statehood or economic revolution?

A Book for Thinkers, Laughers, and Curious Minds

Whether you're a history buff, political junkie, economist, or someone who just loves a good geopolitical "what-if", this book is packed with engaging storytelling, surprising facts, and thoughtful analysis. With a writing style that is as sharp as Arctic winds and as entertaining as a late-night talk show, this book turns serious global politics into an accessible, humorous, and eye-opening adventure.

Is statehood a realistic future for Greenland, or just another American dream? By the time you reach the final chapter, you'll have your own answer—and maybe even a campaign slogan for Greenland's first U.S. senators.

Ready to explore the icy road to statehood?

Grab your parka, buckle up, and dive into one of the most fascinating geopolitical questions of the century.

INTRODUCTION

Greenland – The 51st State? Seriously?
   - Overview of Greenland's current geopolitical landscape
   - Introduction to U.S.-Greenland relations
   - Why the idea of Greenland's statehood is worth exploring
   - The importance of humor in serious discussions

If you're reading this, you've probably asked yourself, "Could Greenland actually become the 51st state of the United States?" Or maybe you just accidentally picked up the wrong book and were looking for something on climate change. Either way—welcome!

Now, I know what you're thinking: Greenland as a U.S. state? That's as likely as Canada invading Florida for warmer beaches! But humor me (literally) because, as far-fetched as this sounds, the idea of Greenland joining the United States has been tossed around more than a snowball in an Arctic blizzard. In fact, it's been seriously considered—by politicians, military strategists, and, yes, even real estate enthusiasts in Washington, D.C. (looking at you, President Truman and President Trump).

So before you dismiss this as another wild conspiracy theory—like Bigfoot being the mayor of a small Alaskan town (which, honestly, wouldn't be the weirdest thing about Alaska)—let's dive into the political, economic, and cultural realities of this hypothetical statehood scenario.

Greenland: A Land of Ice, Opportunity, and Geopolitical Headaches

First things first: Greenland is huge—and I mean massive. It's the world's largest island (sorry, Australia, you're a continent), covering 836,000 square miles—about three times the size of Texas but with fewer people than a Taylor Swift concert. With a population of around 56,000, it's so sparsely populated that your nearest neighbor might actually be a polar bear.

But Greenland's significance isn't just about size—it's about location, resources, and global power struggles. Nestled between North America and Europe, Greenland sits smack-dab in the middle of the Arctic, where melting ice is revealing rich mineral deposits, untapped oil reserves, and new shipping routes that have global superpowers like the U.S., China, and Russia all whispering, "dibs."

For decades, the United States has been eyeing Greenland like a kid in a candy store—except instead of lollipops, the prize is strategic military positioning and Arctic dominance. The U.S. already has a major military presence in Greenland, thanks to Thule Air Base, which has been a key player in missile defense, satellite tracking, and keeping an eye on what Russia is up to when it's not hacking social media accounts.

America and Greenland: A Relationship That's (Mostly) One-Sided

Historically, U.S.-Greenland relations have been a bit like that one overenthusiastic friend who always invites you to their barbecue, even though you've never actually said you'd come.

The U.S. first tried to buy Greenland in 1946 when President Harry Truman offered Denmark $100 million in gold—which, at the time, was the equivalent of trying to buy Manhattan for a few beads and some pocket lint. Denmark said "Nej tak" (No, thanks), and that was the end of that.

Fast forward to 2019, and President Donald Trump casually suggested—on Twitter, of course—that the U.S. should buy Greenland. The idea was met with everything from shock to satire to a very polite but firm NO from Denmark. (They even called it "absurd," which is diplomatic code for "Are you serious?").

But here's the thing: Greenland is more independent than ever. While still technically part of the Kingdom of Denmark, Greenland has its own government and increasing autonomy. And while they rely on Denmark for economic support, they've also been expanding trade ties with other nations, including China, the EU, and—yes—the United States.

So, could Greenland ever voluntarily choose to become part of the U.S.? Well... maybe. The idea isn't as crazy as it sounds when you look at:

-Economic incentives – More U.S. funding, infrastructure, and business opportunities.

-Security and defense – Being part of the U.S. means military protection (and possibly fewer Russian submarines lurking around).

-Greater political influence – Greenland currently has zero seats in the U.S. Congress, but statehood would change that.

But, of course, there are huge challenges as well:

-Loss of cultural identity – Greenlandic Inuit traditions, language, and way of life could be overshadowed.

-Logistical nightmares – Managing a state that's mostly frozen tundra with no highways is... tricky.

-Would Greenlanders even want this? – Spoiler alert: Most don't.

Why This Crazy Idea is Worth Exploring (With a Laugh Along the Way)

So why write a book about something that may never happen? Because thinking through "what-if" scenarios is what political scientists (and conspiracy theorists) do best!

More importantly, this book isn't just about Greenland—it's about the big picture of how nations evolve, how global power shifts, and how history is full of surprises.

After all, Alaska was once Russian territory before the U.S. bought it for a mere $7.2 million in 1867—a move that was called "Seward's Folly" at the time but later proved to be one of the best real estate deals in history. (Except for the Louisiana Purchase, where we got a third of the U.S. for less than the cost of a Super Bowl commercial.)

Could Greenland be the next Alaska? Or is it destined to remain an independent Arctic powerhouse while politely declining America's invitations?

We'll explore that question with humor, history, and a whole lot of political analysis—because, as any good professor knows, the best way to discuss serious topics is to laugh while you do it.

Buckle Up—This Is Going to Be a Wild Ride!

This book will take you on a journey from Viking explorers to Cold War intrigue, from climate change politics to economic power struggles. Along the way, expect plenty of fun facts, historical surprises, and the occasional dad joke—because, let's be honest, we all need a little comic relief when discussing geopolitics.

So grab a warm drink, find a cozy spot, and let's dive into the icy but fascinating world of Greenland: The 51st State?

Oh, and one last fun fact before we start: Did you know Greenland is home to the northernmost McDonald's in the world?

Just kidding. It's not. But if Greenland ever became a U.S. state, I give it six months before a drive-thru pops up next to a glacier.

Let's get started!

GREENLAND'S HISTORY

G reenland's History – More than Just Ice and Vikings
   - Greenland's origins and Norse settlements
   - Denmark's control and modern-day governance
   - Fun fact: Greenland was once "discovered" multiple times!

If history has taught us anything, it's that Greenland is the world's most overachieving iceberg—but also a place of deep historical and geopolitical significance. Long before it became the subject of U.S. land-grab dreams, Greenland was already a place of exploration, survival, and international bargaining.

In this chapter, we'll uncover Greenland's epic origin story, from Viking misadventures to Danish colonial rule to modern-day autonomy—all while answering the big question: How can one island be "discovered" multiple times? (Spoiler: Either explorers didn't leave Yelp reviews, or they just had really bad navigation skills.)

From Ice Age to Vikings: The First Greenlanders

First, let's bust a myth: Erik the Red did NOT discover Greenland. In fact, Greenland was home to Indigenous people thousands of years before the first Viking ever set sail.

The earliest known settlers were the Paleo-Eskimos, who arrived as early as 2500 BCE. They survived on seal hunting, whale blubber, and the ancient Arctic art of "not freezing to death." Over the centuries, different Indigenous cultures, including the Dorset people and later the Thule (ancestors of today's Inuit population), made Greenland their home, adapting to its extreme conditions in ways that make modern-day winter survival look like a vacation.

Then Came the Vikings – And the World's Most Misleading Real Estate Ad

Enter Erik the Red, a Viking outlaw with a talent for both survival and marketing. In 982 AD, Erik was banished from Iceland for some light murder (hey, Vikings had rough tempers). Looking for a fresh start, he set sail west and landed on Greenland's southern coast.

Now, Erik had a problem: He needed settlers, and "Frozen Rock of Doom" wasn't a great sales pitch. So, he did what any good real estate agent would do—he rebranded it. He named it Greenland, thinking people would be more likely to move there. (Yes, that's right—Greenland's name is basically Viking clickbait.)

Surprisingly, it worked! By 985 AD, Erik convinced hundreds of Norse settlers to move to Greenland, where they established two settlements and lived off farming, fishing, and trading.

Unfortunately, Viking life in Greenland wasn't exactly Game of Thrones—it was more Survivor: Arctic Edition. By the 1400s, due to climate change (the Medieval Little Ice Age), isolation, and possibly conflicts with the Inuit, the Norse mysteriously vanished, leaving behind ruins, sagas, and some very confused future historians.

Denmark Takes Over: Greenland, The (Unwanted?) Colony

Fast forward to the 18th century, and Greenland was mostly populated by the Inuit, with occasional European visits. But in 1721, Denmark, under missionary Hans Egede, decided to claim Greenland as its own, bringing Christianity, trade, and (probably) a lot of wool sweaters.

Fun fact: Greenland technically became Danish TWICE.
1. First, as a colony in 1721, when Denmark reasserted control.
2. Then again in 1953, when Denmark made Greenland an official part of the Kingdom.

During this time, Greenland wasn't exactly a priority for Denmark. It was remote, harsh, and had very little economic value beyond fishing and whaling. But its geographic location? That was priceless.

Greenland: The Geopolitical Hotspot (and Frequent Flyer in History Books)

World War II – America's First Big Greenland Crush

During World War II, Denmark was occupied by Nazi Germany—which was problematic for Greenland, since it still relied on Denmark for supplies. The U.S., worried that Germany might take over Greenland's valuable Arctic territory, stepped in to "help."

In 1941, the U.S. established Thule Air Base, an important military outpost that still exists today. This marked America's first serious interest in Greenland—and let's just say, the U.S. never really stopped eyeing the place afterward.

The 1946 Attempted Purchase – The U.S. Tries to Buy Greenland (Again)

After the war, President Harry Truman made Denmark a $100 million offer for Greenland (payable in gold, because America was extra like that). Denmark declined, possibly thinking, "If we said no to the Nazis, we can say no to you."

The 2019 Trump Greenland Incident (Yes, This Happened)

History repeated itself in 2019 when President Donald Trump casually suggested buying Greenland. This time, Denmark responded with sarcasm, and Greenland's government issued a very polite but firm "No, thanks."

Modern Greenland: Autonomy, Identity, and the Future

Today, Greenland is part of the Kingdom of Denmark but has increasing autonomy. In 2009, Greenland gained self-rule, meaning:
* It controls most of its own government functions.
* It can develop its own economy (hello, rare earth minerals).

* It still receives Danish financial support—around $500 million per year.

But Denmark still controls:
* Foreign policy
* Defense & security
* Currency and judiciary

Would Greenland Ever Fully Break Away?

Maybe. Greenlandic political parties have discussed full independence, but there's a catch: Greenland's economy isn't strong enough yet to survive without Denmark's financial aid.

And that brings us back to the big question: Could Greenland ever join the U.S. instead?

- Would it benefit from U.S. funding and economic development?
- Would America's strategic interest in the Arctic make it a priority?
- Would Greenlanders even WANT to become the 51st state?

Those are the questions we'll explore in the coming chapters. But one thing's for sure—history has a funny way of surprising us.

Final Fun Fact: How Many Times Was Greenland "Discovered?"

1. By the Paleo-Eskimos (2500 BCE) – First humans to settle there.

2. By the Norse (982 AD) – Erik the Red "discovered" it, even though people were already living there.

3. By Denmark (1721) – Missionaries and traders "rediscovered" it.

4. By the U.S. (1941 & 1946) – When America "discovered" it was valuable.

5. By Social Media (2019) – When Trump's tweet made Greenland famous again.

At this point, Greenland might hold the world record for Most Rediscovered Place in History.

Now that we've covered how Greenland ended up on the geopolitical map, it's time to look at why the U.S. has been obsessed with it for decades.

Coming up:

- Why the U.S. built a secret Cold War base under the ice (with nuclear missiles, because why not?)

- How Greenland's natural resources could make it a global economic player

- Why modern politicians keep looking at Greenland like it's an Arctic Alaska waiting to happen

AMERICA'S INTEREST IN GREENLAND

A merica's Interest in Greenland – A Love Story in the Making?
- U.S. strategic interests: Military bases and Arctic dominance
    - The 1946 purchase attempt (yes, the U.S. tried to buy Greenland)
    - Current economic ties between the U.S. and Greenland

If there's one thing Americans love, it's real estate. From Louisiana to Alaska to the "fixer-upper" that was Florida in the 1800s, the United States has a history of expanding its borders through strategic purchases and acquisitions. (Fun fact: The U.S. technically bought Alaska from Russia for just $7.2 million—roughly the cost of a downtown Manhattan parking spot today.)

And then, there's Greenland—the icy, resource-rich, strategically located landmass that the U.S. has been eyeing like a long-lost love interest for decades. This is the story of America's not-so-secret Greenland crush, a tale of military strategy, geopolitical intrigue, and one very awkward real estate offer that almost happened in 1946.

Why Is America So Interested in Greenland? (Hint: It's Not for the Sunbathing)

Greenland might not seem like prime real estate—after all, it's covered in 80% ice and has fewer people than some mid-sized cruise ships. But here's the thing: What Greenland lacks in tiki bars, it makes up for in global strategic importance.

1. Location, Location, Location: Greenland as the World's Arctic Highway

Greenland is a geopolitical goldmine, sitting right between North America and Europe. This makes it an ideal military outpost, a strategic Arctic hub, and a gateway to controlling new Arctic shipping routes opening up due to—yep, you guessed it—climate change.

- Military Superpower Playground – The Arctic is heating up (both literally and figuratively) as the U.S., Russia, and China compete for influence in the region.
- Emerging Trade Routes – As ice melts, new shipping lanes are opening, meaning that controlling Greenland is like owning the toll booth on a new highway.
- Proximity to Russia – Greenland is close enough to Russian airspace that the U.S. sees it as an early warning defense post—which is why there's been a U.S. air base there for decades (more on that below).

In short, controlling Greenland is like controlling VIP access to the Arctic Club, and America wants to be on the guest list.

2. America's Military Presence in Greenland: Welcome to Thule Air Base

If you think the U.S. just recently got interested in Greenland, think again. Since World War II, the U.S. has had a military presence in Greenland, and it all started with one crucial location:

Thule Air Base: America's Arctic Stronghold
- Built in 1951, Thule Air Base is the northernmost U.S. military base in the world.
- Originally established to monitor Soviet activity during the Cold War, Thule remains a key early-warning defense station today.
- It's home to a missile defense system, radar tracking, and satellite communications that help the U.S. keep an eye on, well... everything.

Fun Fact: The U.S. once built a secret underground base in Greenland during the Cold War called Camp Century, which was meant to house nuclear missiles under the ice. The plan didn't work out (because, surprise, ice moves), and the whole thing got abandoned—but not before creating one of the weirdest Cold War stories of all time.

The 1946 Purchase Attempt: America's Arctic Shopping Spree

Now, let's talk about one of the boldest (and most unusual) real estate offers in history.

After World War II, America was feeling confident—we had just helped win the war, the economy was booming, and someone in Washington got the idea to buy Greenland.

How It Happened:
- In 1946, President Harry Truman offered Denmark $100 million in gold for Greenland.
- The U.S. was worried about the Soviet Union, and Greenland's location made it a perfect defense outpost.
- Denmark, however, declined—because, well, it's not every day someone tries to buy your territory over coffee and diplomacy.

But the funniest part? Denmark never officially told the Greenlandic people about the offer at the time. Can you imagine waking up one day and finding out your entire homeland was almost sold like a vacation property?

Greenland & the U.S. Today: Economic Ties and Arctic Ambitions

Even though Greenland is still part of Denmark, America hasn't lost interest—and in recent years, U.S.-Greenland relations have gotten even stronger.

1. Economic Partnerships: The U.S. Wants In

Greenland is sitting on a goldmine of natural resources—literally. Underneath all that ice are rare earth minerals, oil, and natural gas.

- The U.S. imported over $500 million in minerals from Greenland in recent years, and American companies want more access to its untapped resources.
- In 2020, the U.S. even opened a consulate in Greenland for the first time in decades, signaling a renewed interest in economic and political partnerships.

2. China's Growing Interest in Greenland (And Why the U.S. Is Nervous)

Here's where things get interesting: China also wants a piece of Greenland.

- China has been investing in mining projects and trying to expand its influence in the Arctic, which makes the U.S. very uncomfortable.
- America's biggest fear? Greenland (and its resources) falling into China's orbit.

This is why the U.S. is stepping up its game—offering more economic aid, investment deals, and trade opportunities with Greenland to keep it away from Chinese influence.

Could America Ever Try to Buy Greenland Again?

Let's be honest: If Greenland were for sale, America would be the first bidder.

- Trump's 2019 Offer: In 2019, President Donald Trump casually suggested buying Greenland—and, once again, Denmark politely but firmly said no.
- Future Possibilities? While Greenland itself isn't interested in U.S. statehood right now, some political experts believe that if

Greenland ever seeks full independence from Denmark, it may look to the U.S. for support.

So, while the idea of Greenland becoming the 51st state may seem far-fetched, the reality is that America's interest in Greenland isn't going anywhere.

Final Thoughts: America & Greenland—A Complicated Relationship

- The U.S. has been interested in Greenland for decades, mainly for military, strategic, and economic reasons.
- America already has a military presence in Greenland, with Thule Air Base still in operation.
- Economic ties between Greenland and the U.S. are growing, especially as the Arctic becomes more important.
- The 1946 and 2019 purchase attempts show that Greenland is more than just an icy afterthought—it's a geopolitical hot spot.

So far, we've talked about why America is interested in Greenland—but what about the other side of the equation?

Would Greenlanders ever WANT to join the U.S.?

WHY WOULD GREENLAND WANT TO JOIN THE U.S.?

W hy Would Greenland Want to Join the U.S.?

Key Points

- The economic pros & cons of joining the U.S.

- Would Greenlanders trade their culture for American benefits?

- Could Greenland become the next Alaska... or would it regret it?

Grab your parka—we're just getting started.

Imagine waking up one morning in Nuuk, Greenland, sipping your coffee, and scrolling through the news—only to see a headline that says:

"Greenland, Welcome to America! Say Hello to the 51st State!"

That's the kind of news that would make anyone choke on their whale blubber jerky.

Now, while the idea of Greenland joining the U.S. might sound as crazy as an igloo in Arizona, it does raise an interesting question:

What's in it for Greenland?

Would statehood bring economic prosperity, political influence, and a modernized future—or would it threaten Greenland's cultural identity and independence?

Let's dive into why (and why not) Greenland might consider swiping right on America's invitation to statehood.

Economic Benefits: The Land of Opportunity (and Federal Funding)

Let's be honest—one of the biggest reasons any region considers statehood is the money. And in Greenland's case, joining the U.S. could be a serious financial game-changer.

1. U.S. Federal Funding: More Money, More Development

Right now, Greenland relies heavily on Denmark for economic support, receiving around $500 million per year in subsidies. While this helps, it's not enough to build the kind of infrastructure Greenland needs for a booming modern economy.

But as a U.S. state, Greenland could receive:
* Billions in federal investment for roads, airports, schools, and hospitals.

* Increased job opportunities in government programs, military bases, and public services.
* Social benefits like Medicare, Social Security, and public education funding.

Just imagine: Greenland finally getting a full-fledged highway system instead of relying on boats, snowmobiles, and the occasional determined sled dog.

2. Economic Growth: Could Greenland Become the "Alaska of the East"?

If Greenland became a state, it could follow in Alaska's footsteps and see a massive boost in economic activity, thanks to:

- Tourism – With U.S. investment, Greenland could become the next big Arctic travel destination (think Iceland 2.0, but with fewer volcanoes and more icebergs).
- Natural Resources – Greenland sits on rich deposits of rare earth minerals, oil, and gas, which could attract major American investment.
- Fishing Industry Expansion – The U.S. could help Greenland expand its fishing industry, making it a major seafood exporter.

Would Greenland become the economic powerhouse of the Arctic? Possibly. Would it also finally get a Starbucks? Almost definitely.

Political Influence: A Small State with a Big Voice

As a territory of Denmark, Greenland currently has little say in global affairs. But as a U.S. state, Greenland would gain a lot more political influence both nationally and internationally.

1. Greenland Would Get Representation in Congress

If Greenland became a state, it would get:

* Two U.S. Senators (which is more than Washington, D.C. has—sorry, D.C.).

* At least one Representative in the House (which, fun fact, is more than Wyoming has in population).

* A direct say in U.S. foreign policy, instead of relying on Denmark's decisions.

Imagine a Greenlandic senator debating Arctic policy in Washington, D.C.—wearing sealskin boots in a room full of people in business suits. Now, that's political representation.

2. More Global Recognition & Strategic Importance

Right now, Greenland is mostly seen as "that big icy place near Canada." But if it became part of the U.S., it would:

- Gain a stronger voice in global politics through U.S. influence.

- Be seen as a key player in Arctic affairs, instead of just a remote island.

- Attract more investment, tourism, and attention from global markets.

Essentially, Greenland would go from being "that big island people forget exists" to being a front-and-center geopolitical player.

Challenges: What Greenland Might Lose in the Deal

Okay, so there are some obvious benefits to joining the U.S. But what's the catch?

Well, becoming a state wouldn't be all sunshine and snowflakes—there are serious downsides to consider.

1. Loss of Cultural Identity: Would Greenland Become "Too American"?

Greenland is home to the Inuit people, whose language, traditions, and way of life have been shaped by thousands of years of Arctic survival.

But joining the U.S. could bring:
* A decline in the Greenlandic language (English would likely become dominant).
* More American cultural influence, possibly diluting traditional Inuit customs.
* Tensions between Greenlanders who embrace Americanization and those who resist it.

Would Greenland keep its strong Indigenous identity, or would it end up with McDonald's, strip malls, and reality TV?

2. Loss of Autonomy: Trading One Government for Another

Right now, Greenland is semi-autonomous—it governs itself in most areas while still relying on Denmark for financial support.

But as a U.S. state, Greenland would have to follow American laws, policies, and federal regulations.

- Greenlanders wouldn't have full control over their resources—the U.S. federal government would have a say.

- Decisions on Greenland's future would be made in Washington, D.C., thousands of miles away.

- Would Greenlanders feel like they truly had a voice, or would they just be another small state in a huge country?

Essentially, Greenland would trade Danish rule for American governance—and that's not necessarily a better deal.

3. Would Greenlanders Even Want This?

Let's get real—most Greenlanders don't seem interested in becoming part of the U.S.

- Polls suggest that Greenlanders value their independence and would rather become fully independent from Denmark than join another country.

- Many fear Americanization would erase their cultural traditions.

- Some Greenlandic leaders have openly rejected U.S. offers for investment, viewing them as attempts to gain influence over Greenland's future.

So, while the economic and political benefits might sound appealing, Greenlanders would have to decide: Is the American Dream worth the trade-offs?

Final Thoughts: A Tempting Offer, But At What Cost?

Would Greenland benefit from U.S. statehood? Yes and no.

- Yes, because:

- Greenland would receive major U.S. investment in infrastructure and social programs.
- It would gain stronger political representation in global affairs.
- It could expand its economy through U.S. trade and business opportunities.

* No, because:
- Greenland would risk losing its unique Inuit identity to American influence.
- It would have less control over its own resources and policies under U.S. federal law.
- Most Greenlanders don't actually want it.

So while statehood might seem like an economic golden ticket, the reality is that Greenland values its independence—and isn't eager to trade it for federal funding and fast food chains.

We've looked at why Greenland might (or might not) want to join the U.S.—but what about the other way around?

- Why is America so interested in Greenland's military value?
- Are Greenland's resources really worth fighting over?
- Would the U.S. actually benefit from a frozen new state?

Let's dive into why Washington, D.C., just can't stop thinking about Greenland.

Grab your snow boots—this is getting interesting.

CHAPTER

4

WHY WOULD THE U.S. WANT GREENLAND?

W hy Would the U.S. Want Greenland?
 - Strategic Arctic military positioning
 - Natural resources: Minerals, fisheries, and ice (just kidding, but not really)
 - Expanding U.S. global influence

Let's play a little game of "Would You Rather?"

Would you rather:
A) Own a massive, strategically located island rich in untapped resources, geopolitical influence, and Arctic dominance?
 OR
B) Let other global superpowers take it while you watch from the sidelines, eating your Freedom Fries?

If you chose A, congratulations—you might be qualified to work in the U.S. State Department!

For decades, Greenland has been one of America's favorite geopolitical obsessions, and not just because it would look amazing on a Risk board. Greenland sits at the intersection of military strategy, economic opportunity, and global power projection—making it a dream acquisition for Washington, D.C.

So, what exactly makes Greenland so irresistible to the U.S.? Let's break it down.

1. Strategic Arctic Military Positioning – Greenland: America's Ice-Cold Aircraft Carrier

If there's one thing history has taught us, it's that the U.S. military loves having a forward position. And Greenland is the Arctic VIP section when it comes to defense, surveillance, and power projection.

Thule Air Base: America's Cold War Bunker (That Never Left)

Let's take a trip back in time to 1951, when the U.S. military built Thule Air Base, the northernmost U.S. base in the world. Originally designed as a Cold War lookout post, Thule has remained a crucial part of America's defense network ever since.

Why? Because Greenland is perfectly positioned for missile detection, early warning systems, and Arctic dominance.

* Missile Defense – Thule's radar system is one of the first lines of defense against any potential ICBM (Intercontinental Ballistic Missile) attacks—especially from that one country that rhymes with "Prussia."

* Surveillance Hub – The base helps track satellites, aircraft, and potential military activity in the Arctic.
* U.S. Military Presence in the Arctic – With climate change opening new Arctic trade routes, Greenland is becoming even more important for America's long-term military strategy.

Fun Fact: The U.S. once had a secret military project under Greenland's ice called Camp Century, where they tried to hide nuclear missiles beneath the Arctic. It failed (because, shocker, ice moves), but it's still one of the wildest Cold War stories out there.

The Arctic: The New Global Battleground?

The Arctic region is heating up (both literally and figuratively), with countries like Russia and China increasing their presence in the area. The U.S. sees Greenland as a key stronghold in keeping American interests in the Arctic strong.

- Russia has been building Arctic military bases and increasing submarine patrols—which makes the Pentagon a little nervous.
- China has been investing in Greenland's mining operations and trying to increase its influence—raising concerns about Chinese economic expansion in the Arctic.
- The U.S.? Well, we'd rather not have to deal with Arctic rivals, which is why keeping Greenland close is a strategic priority.

Would Greenland as a U.S. state make Arctic dominance easier for America? Absolutely.

Would it make Moscow and Beijing happy? Not even a little.

2. Natural Resources: Minerals, Fisheries, and Ice (Yes, Ice!)

While most people look at Greenland and think "giant ice cube", economists and geologists see dollar signs.

Rare Earth Minerals: Greenland's Billion-Dollar Jackpot

Hidden beneath Greenland's frozen surface are massive deposits of rare earth minerals, including:

* Uranium (used for nuclear power and weapons)
* Zinc & Iron (crucial for construction and industry)
* Rare Earth Elements (vital for smartphones, electric cars, and military tech)

Now, here's why the U.S. REALLY cares:

- China currently controls 85% of the world's rare earth mineral production.
- The U.S. wants to reduce its dependence on China for these crucial resources.
- Greenland could be a major supplier of these materials, helping America compete in tech, energy, and defense.

Basically, Greenland is like the Costco of rare minerals, and the U.S. would love a membership card.

Fishing Industry: Greenland's Seafood Goldmine

Greenland's massive fisheries provide some of the best seafood in the world, and the U.S. would love a bigger slice of that market.

- The waters around Greenland are rich with cod, halibut, shrimp, and Arctic char.
- With the melting ice caps opening new fishing areas, the industry is set to expand.

- If Greenland became a U.S. state, it could become a huge supplier to American seafood markets.

Think Alaska, but even colder and with more Viking history.

And Yes... Ice Matters, Too

Sure, we joke about Greenland being just a block of ice, but here's the thing—freshwater reserves are a big deal.

- Greenland holds 10% of the world's freshwater supply.
- As global freshwater shortages increase, Greenland's melting ice could become a valuable export commodity.
- Yes, this means people might someday PAY for Greenlandic ice water. (Let's be honest—some hipster brand will sell it in glass bottles for $10.)

3. Expanding U.S. Global Influence – Because America Never Stops Expanding

Adding Greenland as the 51st state would expand America's reach in ways we haven't seen since we bought Alaska.

1. America's Newest Arctic Powerhouse
If Greenland joined the U.S.:
- America would be one of the largest Arctic nations, rivaling Russia and Canada in Arctic influence.
- The U.S. would control key Arctic shipping routes—which are becoming more valuable every year.
- NATO would gain even stronger Arctic presence, making it harder for Russia and China to increase their foothold in the region.

2. Political Influence in Europe & the Arctic Council

- Right now, Greenland is part of the Kingdom of Denmark, which means it relies on Denmark for foreign policy.

- If Greenland became a U.S. state, it would give America an even bigger say in Arctic Council decisions.

- Denmark's influence in Arctic affairs would shrink, while America's would skyrocket.

Translation: Greenland could be the ultimate power play for expanding U.S. global influence.

Final Thoughts: Is Greenland Worth the Effort?

Would the U.S. benefit from acquiring Greenland?
Yes, because:
- Greenland is a strategic military location that helps U.S. Arctic defense.

- It holds trillions of dollars in untapped natural resources.

- It expands America's influence in Arctic politics and global trade.

* No, because:
- Greenlanders don't seem interested in U.S. statehood.

- Running an Arctic state is expensive—Alaska costs billions in federal spending, and Greenland would be no different.

- It could anger U.S. allies like Denmark and trigger geopolitical tensions.

Would the U.S. love to own Greenland? Of course.

Will it ever happen? That's a whole other question.

Now that we know why the U.S. is interested in Greenland, the next big question is: Could this actually happen?

Buckle up—we're about to get political.

THE POLITICAL PROCESS

The Political Process – Can Greenland Actually Become a State?
- Steps for statehood: The constitutional path
- Precedents from Alaska and Hawaii
- The U.S. Congress and the Greenlandic referendum

If there's one thing Americans love, it's adding more stars to the flag (well, historically speaking—after all, we did it 37 times since 1776).

But could Greenland ever become the 51st star?

Short answer: Maybe.

Long answer: Buckle up, because we're about to take a deep dive into the bureaucratic funhouse that is the U.S. Constitution, historical statehood precedents, and the political hurdles Greenland would face.

And yes, there will be a dad joke along the way. (What did the Constitution say to Greenland? "You better read the fine print!")

1. The Constitutional Path to Statehood – How Does This Actually Work?

Contrary to popular belief, you can't just slap a "For Sale" sign on a country and expect it to become a U.S. state overnight.

Statehood follows a legal and political process—one that is, let's just say, not as simple as ordering a Greenlandic souvenir online.

Step 1: Greenland (or Denmark) Would Have to Propose Statehood

Right now, Greenland is an autonomous territory of Denmark, which means it would need:
* A decision to seek statehood—which could come from either Greenland's government or Denmark (though Greenland is increasingly independent from Danish rule).
* A formal request to the U.S. government—because, let's be real, the U.S. isn't just going to annex Greenland like a lost luggage claim.

Step 2: Greenland Would Hold a Referendum (A Fancy Word for a Vote)

Once the idea is officially on the table, Greenland's citizens would have to vote on whether they actually want to become a U.S. state.

- Fun Fact: Greenland already held a referendum in 2008 that resulted in more autonomy from Denmark, which suggests that full independence is more likely than statehood.

Would Greenlanders vote to join the U.S.?
- Right now, polls suggest that most Greenlanders prefer full independence over joining any other country.
- But if economic hardships or geopolitical pressures (ahem, China and Russia) increase, statehood might become more appealing in the future.

Step 3: The U.S. Congress Would Have to Approve It

This is where things get interesting. According to Article IV, Section 3 of the U.S. Constitution, Congress has the power to admit new states—but only if a majority of both the House and Senate vote YES.

If Greenland somehow convinced the U.S. to take it in, Congress would have to:
* Draft and pass a Statehood Bill, detailing how Greenland would be incorporated into the U.S.
* Agree on financial arrangements, governance structure, and legal issues.
* Deal with any international backlash (looking at you, Denmark).

And let's not forget the BIGGEST debate that would happen in Congress:

Would Greenland be a red state or a blue state?
(Spoiler: If it stays covered in ice, maybe a white state?)

- If one political party thinks Greenland would favor the other, expect statehood debates to drag on longer than a DMV line.
- History has shown that political calculations often delay statehood votes (just ask Puerto Rico).

2. What Can We Learn from Alaska and Hawaii?

Greenland wouldn't be the first faraway, sparsely populated, resource-rich place to become a U.S. state.

Let's take a look at Alaska and Hawaii—the two most recent additions to the United States.

Alaska: The "Ice to Riches" Story

Much like Greenland, Alaska was once viewed as an empty, frozen wasteland (which, let's be honest, is just how people from Florida see anything north of Georgia).

- In 1867, the U.S. bought Alaska from Russia for $7.2 million—a move critics called "Seward's Folly" because, at the time, people thought we paid too much for snow and bears.
- Fast forward to 1959, and Alaska became the 49th state, thanks to its economic potential and military value (sound familiar?).

Would Greenland follow a similar path? Possibly—but Greenland's political culture is different from Alaska's, and it still has ties to Denmark.

Hawaii: The Tropical Exception

Hawaii's journey to statehood was unique because:

- It was an independent kingdom before being annexed by the U.S. in 1898.
- It had a booming economy (thanks to sugar and pineapple plantations).
- It became the 50th state in 1959 after a successful referendum.

Greenland's key difference from Hawaii?

- Hawaii had a strong American presence for decades before statehood.
- Greenland still maintains its own political identity and has fewer economic ties to the U.S.

That being said, both Alaska and Hawaii prove that remote, strategically important places can become states—if the political will exists.

3. The U.S. Congress and International Hurdles

Even if Greenland wanted to become a state, and even if Congress approved, there's one big international problem:

Denmark Would Have a LOT to Say About This

- Greenland is still part of the Kingdom of Denmark.
- Denmark still provides hundreds of millions of dollars in subsidies to Greenland.
- Losing Greenland would weaken Denmark's international influence.

So, how would Denmark react if Greenland suddenly wanted to join the U.S.?

Probably with a strong diplomatic protest, maybe even legal challenges.

(Translation: Denmark would NOT send a "Congrats on Your Statehood" card.)

Would the U.S. risk damaging relations with Denmark for Greenland?

- If Greenland declared independence first, Denmark might have no say in the matter.

- But if the U.S. tried to buy Greenland again (cough 1946, cough 2019), expect some serious international drama.

Final Verdict: Could Greenland Actually Become a U.S. State?

Could it happen? Technically, yes.
Would it be easy? Absolutely not.

For Greenland to join the U.S., it would need:
- Greenlanders to vote for statehood
- The U.S. Congress to approve the move
- A way to resolve Denmark's objections
- Political leaders willing to push for it

Right now, none of these steps seem likely—but history has taught us that politics can be unpredictable.

If economic pressures increase, if Denmark loosens its grip, or if the U.S. becomes more aggressive about Arctic dominance—then maybe, just maybe, Greenland could one day be America's northernmost state.

Now that we've tackled the "Could it happen?" question, let's dive into the "Should it happen?" debate.

Let's weigh the good, the bad, and the frozen.

THE PROS AND CONS OF GREENLANDIC STATEHOOD

The Pros and Cons of Greenlandic Statehood
  - Pros: Economic development, security, and integration
  - Cons: Governance issues, logistical challenges, cultural shifts

Imagine walking into a Greenlandic town hall meeting, where the citizens have gathered to debate whether they should become the 51st state of the United States.

One side says: "Think of the opportunities! More jobs, better infrastructure, and a McDonald's on every corner!"

The other side says: "Do we really want American reality TV and the IRS showing up?"

It's a big decision, and like any major life choice (getting married, moving to a new city, ordering pineapple on pizza), there are pros and cons.

So let's break it down—the good, the bad, and the frozen.

The Pros: Why Greenland Might Say "Yes" to America

If Greenland were to become a U.S. state, there would be some serious perks—economic growth, security, and global influence.

1. Economic Development: From Ice to Industry

Right now, Greenland's economy is heavily dependent on fishing and Danish subsidies. While that's enough to keep the lights on (and the fishing boats running), it doesn't leave much room for growth.

But under U.S. statehood, Greenland could see:
* Billions in federal funding for infrastructure—roads, airports, housing, and energy projects.
* Expanded business and trade opportunities, as American companies invest in mining, tourism, and fisheries.
* Higher-paying jobs, as new industries develop and Greenlanders gain access to the U.S. job market.

Think of Alaska: When it became a state, it gained massive investment from Washington, D.C., turning it from a remote outpost into an economic powerhouse (while keeping its rugged charm).

Could Greenland follow the same path? Absolutely.

2. Security: Welcome to the World's Most Exclusive Military Alliance

Let's be real—being part of the U.S. comes with a major security upgrade.

As a U.S. state, Greenland would:
* Be fully protected by the U.S. military—no more relying on Denmark's limited defense budget.
* Gain more influence in NATO, as an official U.S. state with Arctic strategic importance.
* Benefit from coastal security, emergency response funding, and military infrastructure upgrades.

Right now, the U.S. already has Thule Air Base in Greenland, a key part of its missile defense and Arctic surveillance network. If Greenland became a state, expect more bases, more funding, and more military resources.

Would this make Greenland an even bigger geopolitical target? Maybe—but with the U.S. military behind it, Greenland wouldn't have to worry about fending off foreign threats alone.

3. Political Influence: From Arctic Observer to Global Player

Greenland currently has limited global influence—most major foreign policy decisions are still made by Denmark.

But as a U.S. state, Greenland would:
* Have two U.S. senators (more representation than Washington, D.C. currently has—sorry, D.C.).
* Get at least one representative in Congress, meaning Greenland would have a say in federal laws and policies.
* Gain a bigger voice in Arctic and international affairs—not as a Danish territory, but as a full U.S. state.

Instead of watching from the sidelines, Greenland could be a major player in U.S. foreign policy, trade deals, and environmental negotiations.

The Cons: Why Greenland Might Say "No, Thanks"

Okay, so statehood sounds great on paper, but let's not overlook the potential downsides.

1. Governance Issues: A Bureaucratic Blizzard

Right now, Greenland has a small government that runs things on its own terms.

But as a U.S. state, it would have to deal with:
* Federal oversight from Washington, D.C.—meaning Greenlandic officials wouldn't have as much control.
* American bureaucracy—imagine having to navigate U.S. tax laws, healthcare policies, and endless paperwork.
* New political divisions—Greenland's current government is relatively unified, but as a U.S. state, it would likely see more partisan political battles.

Greenland would go from being an autonomous region with a lot of self-rule to being a state governed under federal laws. Some Greenlanders might see this as a loss of independence, rather than a gain in opportunities.

2. Logistical Challenges: Running a Frozen, Remote State Ain't Cheap

Let's talk about the elephant in the room (or, in this case, the polar bear on the iceberg): Greenland is expensive to manage.

* Infrastructure Costs Would Be Sky-High – Building roads, airports, and energy grids across one of the most extreme climates on Earth would cost billions.

* It's Hard to Get Around – Unlike other U.S. states, Greenland has no roads connecting its towns. Travel is done by boat, plane, or snowmobile—making logistics a nightmare.

* The U.S. Already Struggles With Remote States – Alaska and Hawaii both require heavy federal funding just to stay functional. Greenland would be even more expensive.

Would American taxpayers be willing to spend billions on Greenland's development? Maybe—but they'd probably expect Greenland to generate revenue in return.

3. Cultural Shifts: Will Greenland Stay Greenlandic?

One of the biggest concerns for Greenlanders is preserving their unique Inuit culture, language, and traditions.

* Loss of Language: Greenlandic is the official language, but statehood could mean a push toward English.

* Americanization: U.S. influence could dilute Greenland's Indigenous traditions, as American businesses, entertainment, and politics take over.

* Would Greenland Keep Its Identity? If it became a state, Greenland might struggle to balance its heritage with its new American identity.

This is a major reason why Greenlanders have resisted full integration with Denmark, let alone the U.S. They value their autonomy and cultural uniqueness—and statehood could put that at risk.

Final Verdict: Should Greenland Join the U.S.?

So, after weighing the pros and cons, would statehood be a good move for Greenland?

- Yes, because:
- It would receive massive U.S. investment in infrastructure and economic growth.
- It would gain stronger military protection and global influence.
- It could expand industries like mining, fishing, and tourism, boosting prosperity.

* No, because:
- It might lose some autonomy and cultural identity.
- The logistics of running Greenland as a U.S. state would be incredibly expensive.
- Many Greenlanders prefer independence over joining another country.

Right now, the majority of Greenlanders seem to favor full independence over statehood—but history is full of surprises. If economic pressures shift or geopolitical tensions increase, Greenland's stance on the issue could evolve.

Could we someday see the Stars and Stripes waving over Nuuk?

Maybe. But it wouldn't happen without serious debate, major negotiations, and probably a lot of political drama.

So, if Greenland did become a U.S. state... how would its culture mix with American life?

Let's explore what happens when two VERY different cultures collide.

Grab your popcorn (or dried fish)—this is gonna be fun.

CULTURAL DIFFERENCES

C ultural Differences – Icebergs, Hot Dogs, and American Football?
- How Greenlandic and American cultures compare
- Challenges in cultural integration
- Would Greenlanders accept Americanization?

Imagine walking into a Greenlandic café and seeing a menu that offers seal stew with a side of deep-fried Twinkies.

Or picture a Greenlandic fisherman coming home after a long day on the Arctic waters, cracking open a can of Pepsi, and turning on Monday Night Football.

Now, while these scenarios might sound like something out of a bizarre alternate universe, they bring up a real question:

What would happen if Greenland joined the United States—culturally speaking?

Would Greenlanders embrace American life, or would they cling to their Inuit roots like a walrus on a drifting iceberg? Let's take a deep dive into the clash (or fusion) of cultures between the land of ice and the land of... well, barbecue and reality TV.

How Greenlandic and American Cultures Compare

Before we answer "Would Greenlanders embrace Americanization?", let's take a look at how these two cultures stack up against each other.

Category	Greenland	United States
Population	56,000 (entire country)	330 million (slightly more)
Food	Whale, seal, reindeer, fish	Burgers, hot dogs, pizza
Sports	Soccer, handball, dog sledding	Football, basketball, baseball
Climate	Cold. Very cold. Seriously.	Everything from desert to tundra
Language	Greenlandic (Kalaallisut), Danish	English, Spanish, and more
Driving Style	No roads between cities	Traffic jams for miles
Humor Style	Dry, witty, self-deprecating	Loud, exaggerated, meme-heavy

While Greenland and the U.S. share Western influences, Greenland has maintained a strong Indigenous Inuit identity, with deep connections to hunting, nature, and community life.

The U.S., on the other hand, is a cultural melting pot—which sometimes feels more like a chaotic potluck, where everyone brings their own dish and argues over whose is best.

Challenges in Cultural Integration

So, if Greenland were to become the 51st state, what cultural challenges would it face?

1. Language: English vs. Greenlandic – Would "Howdy" Replace "Aluu"?

Right now, Greenlandic (Kalaallisut) is the official language, and while many people also speak Danish, English isn't widely spoken.

If Greenland became a U.S. state, there would be pressure to adopt English—which might not sit well with Greenlanders who see their language as a crucial part of their identity.

Fun Fact: Greenlandic is a polysynthetic language, meaning you can express an entire sentence in a single word.
For example, "Sukulaatitortarputit" means "You are eating chocolate."
(In the U.S., we just say, "Nice, pass me some.")

Would Greenlanders be okay with learning English, or would the U.S. have to adopt Greenlandic as an official language? (Hint: Congress barely agrees on anything, so don't hold your breath.)

2. Food: From Whale Blubber to French Fries

One of the biggest culture shocks would undoubtedly be food.

* Greenlandic diet: Fresh fish, reindeer, musk ox, seal, whale, and even seabirds.
* American diet: Deep-fried everything, burgers, BBQ, and supersized sodas.

Would Greenlanders trade seal soup for Chick-fil-A? Probably not entirely.

But with an influx of American fast food chains, Greenland could end up seeing a shift toward more processed foods and less traditional Arctic cuisine—which could cause concerns about health and preserving local food traditions.

3. Sports: Would Greenlanders Embrace American Football?

Right now, Greenland's top sports are:
Soccer (Because Europe's influence runs deep)
Handball (A sport wildly popular in Scandinavia)
Dog Sledding (For when the roads run out)

If Greenland became a U.S. state, you can bet that the NFL, NBA, and MLB would try to make inroads—because nothing says "Welcome to America" like a multimillion-dollar sports franchise.

But would Greenlanders embrace American football, or would they stick with their existing sports culture?

(Maybe the compromise would be playing football on ice—who wouldn't want to see Tom Brady try to throw a pass in a snowstorm?)

4. Holidays & Traditions: Would Santa Get the 4th of July Off?

Greenland has its own set of holidays and traditions, including:

December 24 – The main Christmas celebration (a day early compared to the U.S.)

National Day (June 21) – A celebration of Greenlandic culture and independence

Hunting Festivals – Traditions tied to the Inuit way of life

Would Greenlanders adopt the 4th of July, Thanksgiving, or even... Black Friday?

Sure, fireworks are universal—but trading quiet fishing villages for Black Friday stampedes at Walmart? That might be a harder sell.

Would Greenlanders Accept Americanization?

So, here's the million-dollar question:

Would Greenlanders fully embrace American culture, or would they resist it?

Arguments for Integration
- Many Greenlanders already consume American media, music, and entertainment.

- Younger generations might be more open to cultural blending with the U.S.
- Economic opportunities could lead to more American-style businesses opening in Greenland.

Arguments Against Integration

- Strong Inuit identity – Many Greenlanders are deeply tied to their Indigenous culture and traditions.
- Fear of losing autonomy – Greenland has spent years trying to gain more independence from Denmark—why trade that for American governance?
- The pace of change – Even if Greenland became a state, full cultural integration could take generations (if it happened at all).

Would Greenland look like Alaska 2.0? Or would it carve out a unique identity within the U.S., much like Hawaii has?

Only time (and maybe a few Super Bowl parties) would tell.

Final Thoughts: Can Icebergs and Hot Dogs Coexist?

At the end of the day, cultural integration is complicated.

Could Greenland and America blend cultures while keeping Greenland's Inuit heritage intact? Possibly.

Would there be growing pains, awkward moments, and a few confused tourists along the way? Absolutely.

If Greenland ever became the 51st state, it wouldn't just be a political transformation—it would be a cultural one, too.

Would Greenlanders embrace cheeseburgers and baseball?

Would Americans develop a taste for seal stew and dog sledding?

Stranger things have happened. (After all, the U.S. did once put a man on the moon and pineapple on pizza.)

Now that we've talked culture, let's talk money—because adding a new state isn't just about burgers and football, it's also about taxes, infrastructure, and economic feasibility.

Brace yourself—this might be the coldest financial calculation yet.

ECONOMIC IMPLICATIONS

E conomic Implications – Can the U.S. Afford Another State?
- The cost of incorporating Greenland
- Greenland's economy: Fishing, tourism, and potential industries
- Federal budget concerns

"Buying Greenland" sounds like a great idea—until you check the price tag.

Picture this: The United States is at an imaginary real estate auction, and the auctioneer announces:

"Next up for bidding: A strategically located Arctic landmass with abundant natural resources, breathtaking landscapes, and a very low population density!"

The U.S. raises its hand.
Denmark smirks.

Greenland shrugs.

The auctioneer then adds: "Oh, by the way, it's covered in ice, has limited infrastructure, and will cost billions to develop."

And suddenly, even the U.S. Treasury starts sweating.

If Greenland were to become the 51st state, could America afford it?

Would this be an economic windfall like the Louisiana Purchase or a financial headache like trying to build a Starbucks in Antarctica?

Let's break it down, dollar by dollar.

1. The Cost of Incorporating Greenland – Is Uncle Sam Ready for This Bill?

Adding a new state isn't like ordering an extra-large pizza—it requires massive investment in infrastructure, public services, and economic support.

Here's what Greenland would need if it became a U.S. state:

* Transportation Infrastructure – Roads, bridges, highways (which Greenland currently lacks between cities).
* Public Services – Schools, hospitals, law enforcement, fire departments.
* Government Administration – Courts, state legislature, and all those offices with long lines.
* Military & Defense Investment – More bases, coast guard stations, and airstrips.

How Much Would It Cost?

Let's compare with Alaska—a similar remote, Arctic state:
- When Alaska became a state in 1959, it required billions in federal funding over the next few decades.
- Greenland's infrastructure is even less developed than Alaska's was at the time.
- Experts estimate the cost of developing Greenland's infrastructure could exceed $100 billion—before even considering long-term maintenance.

So, the big question:

Would American taxpayers be willing to foot the bill? (Somewhere, a tax accountant just fainted.)

2. Greenland's Economy: Fishing, Tourism, and Future Industries

If Greenland became a state, it wouldn't just be a financial burden—it also has economic potential.

Fishing: Greenland's Seafood Jackpot

Right now, Greenland's biggest industry is fishing, accounting for 90% of its exports.

- Greenland exports large amounts of cod, shrimp, and halibut, making it a major player in the seafood market.
- The U.S. is already a top buyer of Greenlandic seafood—statehood could expand exports even further.

- If the U.S. invested in modernizing Greenland's fishing industry, it could become a seafood powerhouse.

Would Greenland become the next Alaska in terms of fishing exports? Possibly—just with more icebergs.

Tourism: A Potential Arctic Goldmine

Tourism in Greenland is currently small but growing, attracting adventurous travelers who:
    - Want to see icebergs up close (before they melt)
    - Dream of dog sledding across the Arctic
    - Have a strong Instagram game and need new glacier pics

Could Tourism Boom Under U.S. Statehood?

Absolutely! With American investment and marketing, Greenland could:
    * Build better hotels and transportation to accommodate visitors.
    * Develop cruise ship routes (Alaska makes billions off cruise tourism—why not Greenland?).
    * Expand eco-tourism and adventure travel, like Arctic kayaking and Northern Lights viewing.

Would we see a Disney Greenland Resort™? Hopefully not. But statehood could transform Greenland into a top-tier Arctic travel destination.

Mining & Natural Resources: Greenland's Trillion-Dollar Question

Greenland is sitting on a fortune—literally.

Beneath all that ice are rare earth minerals, uranium, zinc, and iron—resources crucial for:
- Smartphones & electronics
- Electric car batteries
- Renewable energy technology

Right now, China dominates the rare earth minerals market (controlling 85% of the world's supply). If Greenland became part of the U.S., it could:
* Reduce America's reliance on China for critical minerals.
* Bring billions in mining investments from American companies.
* Make Greenland a key player in the global supply chain.

The Downside? Environmental Concerns

Greenlanders value sustainability—and large-scale mining could threaten Arctic ecosystems.

So, the U.S. would have to balance economic gain with environmental protection—which, let's be honest, is not always its strong suit (cough oil pipelines cough).

3. Federal Budget Concerns – Would Greenland Drain U.S. Tax Dollars?

Okay, let's talk cold, hard cash.

Would Greenland Be a Financial Asset or a Burden?

The Financial Concerns

- Greenland has a tiny tax base (only 56,000 people—basically the size of a college football stadium).

- U.S. states are required to fund public services, meaning Greenland would rely heavily on federal aid.

- Developing Greenland's infrastructure would cost billions, and it could take decades before it becomes economically self-sufficient.

The Potential Gains

- Tourism, mining, and fisheries could generate significant revenue.

- Greenland's location has immense strategic value, especially for military and trade advantages.

- Long-term investment could turn Greenland into an economic asset, much like Alaska.

Would Greenland eventually pay for itself? Possibly. But it would take decades of U.S. investment to get there.

(Translation: Don't expect Greenland to be handing out free money like a game show anytime soon.)

Final Verdict: Can the U.S. Afford Greenland?

- Yes, because:
- Strategic value – Militarily, it would be an Arctic stronghold.
- Long-term economic potential – Fisheries, tourism, and resources could boost GDP.
- National security benefits – Strengthening U.S. influence in the Arctic would be priceless.

No, because:

- Immediate costs would be enormous – Infrastructure, services, and government expansion would be expensive.
- Greenland's small tax base means it would rely heavily on federal funding.
- Environmental and cultural concerns might outweigh economic benefits.

Right now, Greenland's statehood looks like a long-term investment rather than a quick economic win.

Would it be worth it for America? That depends on whether the U.S. values the Arctic more for strategic reasons or financial ones.

For now, Greenland remains a fascinating "what if" scenario—one that might be more financially complicated than first meets the eye.

Money is one thing—but what about national security?

Time to trade economic spreadsheets for military blueprints. Let's gear up.

MILITARY AND DEFENSE
IMPACTS

M ilitary and Defense Impacts
- The role of Greenland in NATO and U.S. defense strategy
- Impact on Arctic geopolitics
- Would Greenland want U.S. military bases on its soil?

Greenland: America's Arctic Aircraft Carrier?

There's an old saying: "Whoever controls the Arctic, controls the world."

Okay, maybe it's not that old, and maybe I just made it up, but the point still stands: Greenland is a strategic goldmine for military power—and the U.S. knows it.

If Greenland became the 51st state, it wouldn't just be a win for cartographers struggling with map proportions—it would also reshape U.S. defense strategy, Arctic geopolitics, and NATO operations in a big way.

But here's the million-dollar question:

Would Greenland WANT to become America's Arctic stronghold?

Or would the idea of more military bases, fighter jets, and missile defense systems have Greenlanders thinking, "Uh, thanks, but no thanks"?

Let's break it all down—preferably before Russia, China, or a confused polar bear get involved.

1. Greenland's Role in NATO and U.S. Defense Strategy

Right now, Greenland isn't just a scenic block of ice—it's a crucial player in global security, especially for the U.S. and NATO.

Thule Air Base: The Pentagon's Arctic Watchtower

Location: Northern Greenland (a.k.a. "so far north even Santa wouldn't commute")
Function: Early warning radar, missile defense, and satellite tracking
Owner: Technically Greenland, but leased to the U.S. military since 1951

Why is Thule Air Base so important?
- It's part of the U.S. missile defense system, detecting ICBMs (intercontinental ballistic missiles) before they reach North America.

- It's a key surveillance hub—basically, it keeps an eye on Russian military activity in the Arctic.

- It tracks space activity, including satellites and possibly (wink) UFOs.

Fun Fact: During the Cold War, the U.S. tried to build an entire underground nuclear missile base in Greenland (Project Iceworm), but it failed because—surprise!—ice moves.

If Greenland became a U.S. state, Thule would likely be expanded, making it an even bigger part of America's Arctic defense strategy.

Would this make the U.S. safer? Absolutely.

Would Greenlanders be thrilled about having more military operations on their land? That's another question.

2. Impact on Arctic Geopolitics – The Cold War Isn't Over, It's Just Colder

You might think the Arctic is just a frozen wasteland where nothing happens, but in reality, it's one of the most hotly contested regions on Earth.

The Arctic: The New Global Battleground

If Greenland became a U.S. state, it would:
* Give the U.S. a bigger footprint in Arctic politics.
* Strengthen NATO's northern defense.
* Cause major geopolitical headaches for Russia and China.

1. Russia's Arctic Ambitions – Moscow Won't Be Happy

- Russia has been expanding its Arctic military presence, building new bases, airstrips, and even conducting war games in the region.

- If Greenland became a U.S. state, Russia would see it as a direct threat—leading to even more military buildup in the Arctic.

- Expect strong Russian opposition in the form of diplomatic protests, military exercises, and angry press conferences.

2. China's Quiet Influence – The "Near-Arctic" Power?

- China calls itself a "near-Arctic state" (which is like Florida calling itself "near-Canada," but okay).

- Beijing has been investing in Greenland's mining industry, hoping to secure rare earth minerals and other resources.

- If Greenland joined the U.S., China would likely lose economic influence in the region—which could escalate tensions between Washington and Beijing.

3. NATO's Arctic Power Move

- Right now, Greenland is part of the Kingdom of Denmark, which is a NATO member.

- If Greenland became a U.S. state, NATO's Arctic presence would be significantly strengthened.

- This could pressure Russia into increasing its own military activity—creating a new Cold War dynamic in the Arctic.

Would Greenland's statehood make the Arctic safer or more dangerous? That depends on whether the U.S. and Russia decide to play nice—or play war games.

(Spoiler: They usually don't play nice.)

3. Would Greenland Want More U.S. Military Bases?

Now, let's get to the big question:

Would Greenlanders be okay with more U.S. military presence on their land?

Arguments in Favor of Military Expansion

- Economic Benefits – Military bases bring jobs, infrastructure, and federal funding.
- Increased Security – More U.S. military presence would protect Greenland from foreign threats.
- Improved Arctic Research & Tech – The U.S. could invest in scientific projects alongside defense operations.

Arguments Against More Bases

* Loss of Greenlandic Sovereignty – Greenland has been moving toward full independence, and more U.S. bases could feel like a step backward.
* Environmental Concerns – Military operations could harm Arctic ecosystems, affecting wildlife, fishing, and climate balance.
* Greenland's History with Military Tensions – In the past, Greenlanders have protested U.S. military expansion, fearing it would turn their island into a Cold War chess piece.

Fun Fact: The U.S. accidentally lost a nuclear bomb in Greenland in 1968 when a B-52 bomber crashed near Thule Air Base.

(Don't worry, they cleaned it up... mostly.)

So, while some Greenlanders might welcome the economic benefits of military expansion, others could resist turning their homeland into a giant airstrip.

Would Greenland want to be the "Alaska of the East" when it comes to military importance?

Or would they push back against increased U.S. defense operations?

(Stay tuned for that referendum...)

Final Verdict: Military Dream or Geopolitical Nightmare?

- Yes, because:
- Greenland's statehood would strengthen U.S. Arctic defense.
- It would increase NATO's influence in the region, countering Russia and China.
- The U.S. could invest in Greenland's security, economy, and infrastructure.

* No, because:
- Greenlanders might not want more military presence on their land.
- Russia and China would see it as a provocation, increasing tensions.
- Environmental and sovereignty concerns could lead to major protests.

Would the U.S. benefit militarily from Greenland's statehood? Absolutely.

Would Greenlanders be thrilled about it? That's a lot less certain.

For now, Greenland remains a strategic Arctic gem—one that everyone wants, but no one fully owns.

We've covered military bases, missile defense, and geopolitical rivalries—but let's not forget one crucial thing: Greenland's environment is changing fast.

Grab your eco-friendly coffee cups—we're diving into the environmental side of statehood next.

ENVIRONMENTAL CONCERNS

Environmental Concerns – Melting Ice and Oil Drilling
- Climate change and Greenland's melting glaciers
- Natural resource exploitation risks
- U.S. environmental policies vs. Greenland's sustainability goals

If Greenland were to become the 51st state, it wouldn't just be another spot on the U.S. map—it would be the first state actively melting while we debate what to do with it.

That's right. Greenland is literally disappearing, thanks to climate change. If global warming continues at this pace, future generations might not argue over whether Greenland should be part of the U.S.—but whether it will even exist above sea level.

So, what happens when melting glaciers, oil drilling, and environmental policies collide in Greenland's future?

Would U.S. statehood help protect Greenland's fragile ecosystem, or would it turn into the next Texas—just with fewer cowboy hats and more icebergs?

Let's dig into the chilling reality of Greenland's environmental concerns (pun 100% intended).

1. Climate Change and Greenland's Melting Glaciers

Here's a fact that's cooler than an Arctic breeze but also terrifying:

- Greenland is losing about 280 billion tons of ice per year.

For context, that's like pouring 112 million Olympic-sized swimming pools worth of ice water into the ocean annually—which, as you can imagine, is not great for sea levels.

Why is Greenland Melting So Fast?

- Global Warming – Rising temperatures are causing Greenland's glaciers to melt at an unprecedented rate.
- Warmer Ocean Currents – The surrounding waters are heating up, accelerating ice loss from below.
- Arctic Amplification – The Arctic is warming twice as fast as the rest of the planet, making Greenland ground zero for climate change.

What Happens if Greenland's Ice Sheet Disappears?

Global sea levels would rise by 23 feet (which, let's be honest, would make Florida's beachfront properties a little too beachfront). Weather patterns would shift, leading to stronger hurricanes, droughts, and food shortages worldwide. Greenland's own communities would suffer flooding and coastal erosion, forcing some villages to relocate entirely.

Fun Fact: If you ever wanted a beachfront home in Nebraska, just wait 100 years. (At this rate, we'll have "Great Plains Beach Resorts" in no time.)

2. Natural Resource Exploitation Risks – Greenland's Arctic Gold Rush

Now, here's where things get interesting. While Greenland's ice is melting, its hidden treasures are being revealed.

Beneath Greenland's glaciers are some of the most valuable untapped natural resources on Earth, including:

* Rare Earth Minerals – Used in smartphones, electric cars, and military tech (China currently dominates this market, so the U.S. is very interested).
* Oil and Gas – Estimated to be billions of barrels worth, sitting under the seabed (hello, energy companies!).
* Uranium and Other Metals – Crucial for nuclear power, construction, and space technology.

With resources like these, Greenland could become a global economic powerhouse—but at what cost?

The Risks of Large-Scale Resource Extraction

* Environmental Damage – Mining operations could destroy Arctic ecosystems, harming wildlife like polar bears, whales, and reindeer.

* Water Contamination – Chemical runoff from mining could pollute Greenland's rivers and ocean waters.

* Cultural Impact – Many Greenlandic communities rely on traditional hunting and fishing, which could be disrupted by industrial expansion.

Would Greenland be willing to sacrifice its pristine environment for economic growth?

And, more importantly, would the U.S. prioritize Greenland's environmental protection—or treat it like another Texas oil field?

(I can already hear the political debates brewing... "Drill, baby, drill" vs. "Save the ice, save the world!")

3. U.S. Environmental Policies vs. Greenland's Sustainability Goals

If Greenland became a U.S. state, it would face a major question:

- Would it have to follow U.S. environmental policies, or could it set its own rules?

How the U.S. Handles Environmental Protection (or Sometimes Doesn't)

In theory, the U.S. has strong environmental protections, such as:

- The Clean Air Act & Clean Water Act – Designed to regulate pollution.
- The Environmental Protection Agency (EPA) – Oversees environmental policies nationwide.
- National Park Protections – Preserving land from industrial development.

But Here's the Reality:

Environmental policies flip-flop depending on who's in office.

Some states (like California) have strict environmental laws, while others (like Texas) are more industry-friendly.

The fossil fuel industry lobbies hard to keep energy policies favorable for oil drilling.

Would Greenland get the California treatment (strict laws and green energy focus) or the Texas treatment (drill first, ask questions later)?

(Knowing U.S. politics, probably both, depending on the election year.)

4. Would Greenland Want U.S. Environmental Policies?

Right now, Greenland's government has strict environmental protections—but as a U.S. state, it might lose some of that autonomy.

Greenland's Current Environmental Goals
Sustainability First – Greenland prioritizes long-term ecological health over short-term profit.

Global Climate Leadership – It has been a major voice in Arctic climate talks, pushing for international action.

Protecting Indigenous Traditions – Many Inuit communities rely on sustainable hunting and fishing, which could be threatened by industrial expansion.

Potential Conflicts with U.S. Policies

* The U.S. might push for more mining and oil drilling to compete with China and Russia.

* Greenland might have to fight for stricter environmental laws to protect its way of life.

* The U.S. could prioritize economic growth over climate concerns, leading to local resistance from Greenlanders.

Would Greenland trust Washington, D.C. to protect its environment—or would it feel like another forgotten state when political priorities shift?

Final Verdict: Can Greenland Balance Growth with Environmental Protection?

- Yes, because:
- Greenland has strict environmental protections in place.
- U.S. statehood could bring green energy investments to replace fossil fuels.
- America has some of the strongest environmental laws in the world (when enforced).

* No, because:
- U.S. politics change frequently, meaning environmental policies aren't always stable.
- Greenland's economy would be pressured to expand resource extraction, even at ecological costs.

- Greenlanders might lose control over their own environmental decisions under U.S. federal law.

Would Greenland as a U.S. state be a climate success story—or an Arctic cautionary tale?

For now, Greenland is walking a fine line between economic opportunity and environmental responsibility.

If statehood ever happens, it will need to fight hard to keep its glaciers intact—before they melt into history.

We've covered the politics, economy, military strategy, and environment—but what about the people who actually live in Greenland?

Would Greenlanders even vote to join the U.S.—or would they prefer independence?

Time to check the political temperature in Nuuk (and yes, it's still cold).

HOW WOULD
GREENLANDERS VOTE?

H ow Would Congress React?
 - Republican vs. Democratic perspectives
- Potential legislative hurdles
- The role of international treaties and Denmark's response

If Greenland somehow voted "Yes" on becoming the 51st state, the next question would be: What would Congress say?

Would lawmakers in Washington, D.C. welcome Greenland with open arms—or would they bury the idea under 1,000 pages of legal jargon and political bickering?

Well, if history has taught us anything, it's that Congress loves a good debate—especially when it involves new states, foreign policy, and the potential for unlimited snow cones.

Let's break it down: How would Democrats and Republicans react? What legislative roadblocks would Greenland face? And would Denmark throw a diplomatic snowball at us for trying?

1. Republican vs. Democratic Perspectives – Would Either Party Support Greenlandic Statehood?

Imagine a heated debate on the floor of Congress, where senators and representatives are passionately arguing about... Greenland.

Some might see it as a strategic goldmine, while others might say, "Do we really need more ice?"

So how would the two major U.S. political parties react?

Republican Perspective: "What's in it for us?"

Republicans might oppose Greenlandic statehood for several reasons:
* Would Greenland vote Democrat? If Greenland were projected to elect Democratic senators and representatives, Republicans would likely resist adding a new blue state to the map. (See: Puerto Rico debates.)
* Fiscal Concerns – Greenland would require massive federal investment in infrastructure and public services—something small-government conservatives might oppose.
* Foreign Policy Risks – Some Republicans might worry that annexing Greenland would escalate tensions with Denmark, NATO, Russia, and China.

But Republicans might support Greenlandic statehood if:

* Strategic Military Advantages – More U.S. military presence in the Arctic could counter Russia and China's growing influence in the region.

* Economic Potential – If Greenland's rare earth minerals and energy reserves could benefit U.S. businesses, some Republicans might see it as an investment.

* Arctic Energy Resources – Greenland has huge oil and gas reserves—and certain Republican leaders might favor energy independence over environmental concerns.

Best-case scenario for Republicans: If Greenland somehow became a Republican-leaning state (unlikely, but hypothetically possible), they might be all in on adding it to the union.

Democratic Perspective: "Statehood Sounds Great, But..."

Democrats might support Greenlandic statehood for reasons like:

* More Global Influence – Having Greenland in the U.S. would increase American power in the Arctic and strengthen NATO.

* Green Energy Investments – Greenland is rich in wind, hydro, and rare earth minerals needed for green technology—a perfect fit for Democratic climate policies.

* Potentially More Democratic Votes – Since Greenland's political culture leans left, it's likely to elect Democratic senators and representatives.

But Democrats might oppose Greenlandic statehood because:

* Huge Federal Spending Requirements – Funding roads, airports, healthcare, and education in Greenland would be incredibly expensive—and some Democrats might hesitate at expanding the budget even further.

* Indigenous & Environmental Concerns – Greenland's Inuit population could resist Americanization, and many Democrats would want to respect Indigenous sovereignty.

* Complicated Diplomatic Issues – A Democratic administration might avoid disrupting U.S.-Denmark relations—especially since Denmark is a key NATO and EU ally.

Best-case scenario for Democrats: If Greenland aligned with progressive climate and Indigenous policies, Democrats might push for statehood as a long-term geopolitical win.

2. Legislative Hurdles – Why Congress Might Stall (Forever)

Even if both political parties found some common ground (which, let's be real, is about as rare as a warm day in Greenland), there would still be serious legal and legislative roadblocks.

The Constitutional Process – Can Congress Even Add Greenland?

The U.S. Constitution (Article IV, Section 3) states that Congress can admit new states—but it doesn't say how fast that process has to happen. (Spoiler: It can take decades.)

Major Hurdles to Greenlandic Statehood

Congress Would Need a Majority Vote – Both the House of Representatives and the Senate would have to approve Greenland's statehood.

Denmark Would Have to Agree (Or Greenland Would Have to Declare Independence) – More on this below, but international treaties matter.

Negotiating Federal & State Laws – Greenland would need a state constitution, new legal systems, and integration into U.S. law—a process that took years for Hawaii and Alaska.

Budget Approval for Greenland's Development – Greenland lacks infrastructure, meaning Congress would have to approve billions in federal spending—something that's always a hot debate.

How long could this process take?

- Alaska & Hawaii took nearly 50 years from purchase to statehood.

- Puerto Rico has been debating statehood for decades with no resolution.

- Greenland could be tied up in Congress for years—if not longer.

(Translation: Greenlandic statehood could be stuck in more red tape than an unopened Christmas present.)

3. The Role of International Treaties & Denmark's Response

Now, let's talk about the diplomatic elephant in the room: Denmark.

Would Denmark Allow Greenland to Join the U.S.?

Right now, Greenland is an autonomous territory of Denmark. That means:

Denmark still technically owns Greenland.

Greenland would need either Denmark's approval OR full independence first.

International treaties (including NATO agreements) would complicate things.

Denmark's likely reaction to a U.S. statehood bid for Greenland?

* Strong opposition. Denmark has rejected past U.S. attempts to buy Greenland (1946, 2019).
* Legal barriers. Denmark could challenge any U.S. move under international law.
* Economic concerns. Losing Greenland would mean losing Danish financial interests, Arctic influence, and strategic positioning.

But...

* If Greenland became fully independent first, Denmark wouldn't have a say.
* If the U.S. made an irresistible offer, Denmark might consider negotiating.
* If geopolitical tensions escalated, Denmark could change its mind for security reasons.

Would the U.S. risk damaging relations with Denmark and NATO for Greenland?

Probably not—unless the geopolitical stakes were high enough.

Final Verdict: Would Congress Approve Greenlandic Statehood?

- Yes, if...

- Greenland had a clear pro-statehood vote.

- The U.S. saw major economic and military advantages.

- Denmark either approved or Greenland gained independence first.

* No, because...

- The U.S. rarely acts fast on statehood issues.

- Republicans and Democrats would likely argue over political control.

- Denmark and NATO could strongly oppose the move.

Final Answer?

If Greenland somehow applied for statehood today, Congress would probably debate it for years without taking real action.

(After all, Puerto Rico has been waiting for decades... and it doesn't even have glaciers to melt in frustration.)

What if Greenland didn't want statehood at all?

Time to explore Greenland's Plan B—or as they say in Danish, Alternative B.

HOW WOULD CONGRESS REACT?

H ow Would Congress React?
- Republican vs. Democratic perspectives
- Potential legislative hurdles
- The role of international treaties and Denmark's response

If Greenland somehow voted "Yes" on becoming the 51st state, the next question would be: What would Congress say?

Would lawmakers in Washington, D.C. welcome Greenland with open arms—or would they bury the idea under 1,000 pages of legal jargon and political bickering?

Well, if history has taught us anything, it's that Congress loves a good debate—especially when it involves new states, foreign policy, and the potential for unlimited snow cones.

Let's break it down: How would Democrats and Republicans react? What legislative roadblocks would Greenland face? And would Denmark throw a diplomatic snowball at us for trying?

1. Republican vs. Democratic Perspectives – Would Either Party Support Greenlandic Statehood?

Imagine a heated debate on the floor of Congress, where senators and representatives are passionately arguing about... Greenland.

Some might see it as a strategic goldmine, while others might say, "Do we really need more ice?"

So how would the two major U.S. political parties react?

Republican Perspective: "What's in it for us?"

Republicans might oppose Greenlandic statehood for several reasons:
* Would Greenland vote Democrat? If Greenland were projected to elect Democratic senators and representatives, Republicans would likely resist adding a new blue state to the map. (See: Puerto Rico debates.)
* Fiscal Concerns – Greenland would require massive federal investment in infrastructure and public services—something small-government conservatives might oppose.
* Foreign Policy Risks – Some Republicans might worry that annexing Greenland would escalate tensions with Denmark, NATO, Russia, and China.

But Republicans might support Greenlandic statehood if:

* Strategic Military Advantages – More U.S. military presence in the Arctic could counter Russia and China's growing influence in the region.

* Economic Potential – If Greenland's rare earth minerals and energy reserves could benefit U.S. businesses, some Republicans might see it as an investment.

* Arctic Energy Resources – Greenland has huge oil and gas reserves—and certain Republican leaders might favor energy independence over environmental concerns.

Best-case scenario for Republicans: If Greenland somehow became a Republican-leaning state (unlikely, but hypothetically possible), they might be all in on adding it to the union.

Democratic Perspective: "Statehood Sounds Great, But..."

Democrats might support Greenlandic statehood for reasons like:

* More Global Influence – Having Greenland in the U.S. would increase American power in the Arctic and strengthen NATO.

* Green Energy Investments – Greenland is rich in wind, hydro, and rare earth minerals needed for green technology—a perfect fit for Democratic climate policies.

* Potentially More Democratic Votes – Since Greenland's political culture leans left, it's likely to elect Democratic senators and representatives.

But Democrats might oppose Greenlandic statehood because:

* Huge Federal Spending Requirements – Funding roads, airports, healthcare, and education in Greenland would be incredibly expensive—and some Democrats might hesitate at expanding the budget even further.

* Indigenous & Environmental Concerns – Greenland's Inuit population could resist Americanization, and many Democrats would want to respect Indigenous sovereignty.

* Complicated Diplomatic Issues – A Democratic administration might avoid disrupting U.S.-Denmark relations—especially since Denmark is a key NATO and EU ally.

Best-case scenario for Democrats: If Greenland aligned with progressive climate and Indigenous policies, Democrats might push for statehood as a long-term geopolitical win.

2. Legislative Hurdles – Why Congress Might Stall (Forever)

Even if both political parties found some common ground (which, let's be real, is about as rare as a warm day in Greenland), there would still be serious legal and legislative roadblocks.

The Constitutional Process – Can Congress Even Add Greenland?

The U.S. Constitution (Article IV, Section 3) states that Congress can admit new states—but it doesn't say how fast that process has to happen. (Spoiler: It can take decades.)

Major Hurdles to Greenlandic Statehood

Congress Would Need a Majority Vote – Both the House of Representatives and the Senate would have to approve Greenland's statehood.

Denmark Would Have to Agree (Or Greenland Would Have to Declare Independence) – More on this below, but international treaties matter.

Negotiating Federal & State Laws – Greenland would need a state constitution, new legal systems, and integration into U.S. law—a process that took years for Hawaii and Alaska.

Budget Approval for Greenland's Development – Greenland lacks infrastructure, meaning Congress would have to approve billions in federal spending—something that's always a hot debate.

How long could this process take?

- Alaska & Hawaii took nearly 50 years from purchase to statehood.

- Puerto Rico has been debating statehood for decades with no resolution.

- Greenland could be tied up in Congress for years—if not longer.

(Translation: Greenlandic statehood could be stuck in more red tape than an unopened Christmas present.)

3. The Role of International Treaties & Denmark's Response

Now, let's talk about the diplomatic elephant in the room: Denmark.

Would Denmark Allow Greenland to Join the U.S.?

Right now, Greenland is an autonomous territory of Denmark. That means:

Denmark still technically owns Greenland.

Greenland would need either Denmark's approval OR full independence first.

International treaties (including NATO agreements) would complicate things.

Denmark's likely reaction to a U.S. statehood bid for Greenland?

* Strong opposition. Denmark has rejected past U.S. attempts to buy Greenland (1946, 2019).
* Legal barriers. Denmark could challenge any U.S. move under international law.
* Economic concerns. Losing Greenland would mean losing Danish financial interests, Arctic influence, and strategic positioning.

But...

* If Greenland became fully independent first, Denmark wouldn't have a say.
* If the U.S. made an irresistible offer, Denmark might consider negotiating.
* If geopolitical tensions escalated, Denmark could change its mind for security reasons.

Would the U.S. risk damaging relations with Denmark and NATO for Greenland?

Probably not—unless the geopolitical stakes were high enough.

Final Verdict: Would Congress Approve Greenlandic Statehood?

- Yes, if...

- Greenland had a clear pro-statehood vote.

- The U.S. saw major economic and military advantages.

- Denmark either approved or Greenland gained independence first.

* No, because...

- The U.S. rarely acts fast on statehood issues.

- Republicans and Democrats would likely argue over political control.

- Denmark and NATO could strongly oppose the move.

Final Answer?

If Greenland somehow applied for statehood today, Congress would probably debate it for years without taking real action.

(After all, Puerto Rico has been waiting for decades... and it doesn't even have glaciers to melt in frustration.)

What if Greenland didn't want statehood at all?

Time to explore Greenland's Plan B—or as they say in Danish, Alternative B.

WHAT IF GREENLAND SAID NO?

W hat If Greenland Said No?
　　　　- Potential alternative partnerships
　　- Greenland's future outside the U.S.
　　- The role of the EU and NATO

So, after all this talk about Greenland becoming the 51st state, what if the people of Greenland just looked at the U.S. offer and said…

"No, thanks. We're good."

No fireworks. No flag redesign. No Greenland-themed Fourth of July BBQs (although I'd personally love to see an "Arctic Hot Dog" on the menu).

If Greenland rejected U.S. statehood, what would its future look like?

Would it stay with Denmark, seek total independence, or form new partnerships with the European Union, NATO, or even China?

Let's explore Greenland's Plan B (or Plan Iceberg, if you will).

1. Potential Alternative Partnerships – Who Else Wants to Date Greenland?

If Greenland doesn't want to be the United States' Arctic sweetheart, it still has plenty of other suitors.

Let's take a look at who's courting Greenland and what each potential partnership might mean.

Option 1: Stay with Denmark – "Better the Devil You Know"

Greenland is currently an autonomous territory within the Kingdom of Denmark. That means:
* Greenland controls most of its internal affairs (education, policing, economy).
* Denmark still provides financial aid (about $500 million per year—nearly half of Greenland's budget).
* Denmark handles foreign policy and defense, meaning Greenland doesn't need to fund its own military.

Would Greenland consider staying with Denmark indefinitely?

Pros:

- Financial Stability – No need to stress about where the money's coming from.

- Strong Ties to the West – As part of Denmark, Greenland remains linked to the EU and NATO.

- Less Political Risk – Independence or statehood could bring economic uncertainty.

Cons:

* Less Political Freedom – Denmark still has the final say on foreign policy.

* Growing Independence Movement – Many Greenlanders want full self-rule.

* Limited Economic Growth – Some believe Denmark's financial aid is holding Greenland back from becoming self-sufficient.

Staying with Denmark is the safe option, but for how long? Greenland's independence movement is growing, meaning this relationship could have an expiration date.

Option 2: Full Independence – Greenland as Its Own Country

Many Greenlanders dream of full independence—but could Greenland actually survive on its own?

Challenges of Greenlandic Independence

Money, Money, Money – Greenland would lose Denmark's annual subsidies, meaning it would need a self-sustaining economy fast.

Defense & Security – Greenland would have to create its own military or rely on international alliances.

Diplomatic Recognition – Becoming an independent country isn't just about declaring it—Greenland would need global recognition.

Could Greenland Make It Work?

If Greenland developed its economy, increased trade, and built strong diplomatic partnerships, it could eventually become self-sufficient.

Successful examples:
* Iceland – A tiny Arctic island nation that gained independence and thrived.
* Singapore – A small but resourceful country that became an economic powerhouse.

Less successful examples:
* South Sudan – Struggled post-independence due to economic instability and weak governance.

Greenland would need a solid economic plan before taking the leap—but full independence could happen within decades.

(At the very least, Greenland's flag would stop being confused for Denmark's.)

Option 3: The European Union – Rejoining the Club?

Believe it or not, Greenland used to be part of the European Union—but in 1985, it became the first and only territory to leave the EU (Brexit before Brexit).

Why did Greenland leave?

- Greenlanders were unhappy with EU fishing policies that hurt their economy.
- They wanted more control over their natural resources.

Could Greenland rejoin the EU in the future?

Pros:
- Access to EU markets and trade agreements.
- Financial aid programs for small nations.
- Greater global influence.

Cons:
* Would have to follow EU regulations (which led to the first breakup).
* Might struggle to have strong political influence in a union with much bigger nations.

Rejoining the EU isn't impossible, but Greenland would have to negotiate favorable terms to protect its economy.

(Translation: The EU would need to promise not to mess with the fish again.)

Option 4: Strengthen NATO Ties – The Military Route

Greenland is already a NATO territory (through Denmark), meaning it benefits from Western military protection.

If Greenland became independent, would it strengthen its NATO partnership?

Benefits of a NATO-focused strategy:

- Security Without Needing a Full Military – NATO could defend Greenland from potential threats.

- Closer Ties to the U.S. & Europe – Strengthening Greenland's strategic role in the Arctic.

- Economic Incentives – NATO investments could help fund infrastructure projects and military bases.

Potential Downsides:
* Would still rely on foreign countries for defense.
* Could become a pawn in U.S.-Russia tensions.

If Greenland wants security without statehood, NATO could be a smart alternative to joining the U.S.

(Because let's be honest—Greenland does NOT want to start its own Air Force from scratch.)

Option 5: China – A Sneaky New Ally?

China has been quietly investing in Greenland's mining and infrastructure projects—which has made both Denmark and the U.S. very nervous.

China sees Greenland as:
- A source of rare earth minerals that China could dominate.
- A strategic Arctic location to expand its influence.
- A potential trade partner if Greenland gains independence.

Would Greenland ever fully align with China? Probably not—Greenlanders generally prefer Western ties.

But China's growing economic interest in Greenland means that, at the very least, Greenland has a backup option if Western partnerships don't work out.

(Let's just say Washington would NOT be happy if Greenland suddenly started using the yuan instead of the Danish krone.)

2. Greenland's Future Outside the U.S. – A Realistic Outlook

So, if Greenland doesn't become the 51st state, what's the most likely future scenario?

Short-term: Stay with Denmark while building up its economy and governance.
Mid-term: Push for greater autonomy and reduce dependence on Denmark's financial aid.
Long-term: Either pursue full independence or develop stronger partnerships with NATO, the EU, or other global powers.

Greenland's best bet? A slow and steady path toward self-sufficiency—without rushing into statehood or independence before it's ready.

(Because let's be honest—no one wants an independence hangover like Brexit.)

Final Verdict: If Not the U.S., Then Who?

- Greenland could thrive without U.S. statehood—but it would need strong economic and security partnerships.
- Denmark remains Greenland's most stable option—but full independence isn't off the table.

- The EU, NATO, and even China could all play a role in Greenland's future—whether the U.S. likes it or not.

Would Greenland ever regret rejecting statehood?

Possibly—but if history has shown us anything, Greenland likes to do things on its own icy terms.

(And honestly, can you blame them? Who wouldn't want to be their own boss?)

But what if Greenland actually did vote for U.S. statehood?

Time to imagine Greenland's American future.

WHAT IF GREENLAND SAID YES?

What If Greenland Said Yes?
  - Transition period: What it would look like
- Potential timeline and integration strategies
- Changes to Greenlandic governance

After all the debates, referendums, and long-winded speeches from politicians (most of which would start with "My fellow Americans... and Greenlanders"), Greenland surprises the world and votes YES to becoming the 51st state of the United States.

Now what?

Would Washington throw a statehood party complete with fireworks and an ice sculpture of the Greenlandic flag?

Would Greenland suddenly be filled with Walmarts, drive-thrus, and enthusiastic campaign stops from presidential candidates who can't pronounce "Kalaallit Nunaat"?

Not quite. Turning Greenland into a U.S. state wouldn't happen overnight. It would take years—if not decades—of transition.

Let's explore what the process would look like, how long it would take, and how Greenland's governance would change under the Stars and Stripes.

1. The Transition Period – What Happens After the Vote?

The moment Greenlanders say "Yes" to statehood, the U.S. government would enter full bureaucratic mode.

(Think: mountains of paperwork, endless congressional debates, and at least one dramatic Senate filibuster.)

Here's what would need to happen:

Step 1: Congress Must Approve Greenland's Statehood Bill

According to the U.S. Constitution (Article IV, Section 3), Congress has the power to admit new states—but only if both the House of Representatives and the Senate vote in favor.

Potential obstacles:
- Would Republicans and Democrats agree on adding a new state?
- Would Denmark object or demand compensation?
- Would existing U.S. states complain about sharing federal funding with Greenland?

If Congress approved the bill, Greenland would officially enter the transition phase.

(At this point, Greenland might start getting "Welcome to America" gift baskets from all 50 governors.)

Step 2: The "Territorial Phase" – Greenland Becomes a U.S. Territory First

Before becoming a state, Greenland would likely spend several years as a U.S. territory, similar to Puerto Rico or Guam.

- What changes immediately?
* Greenlandic citizens would gain U.S. passports and become U.S. nationals.
* Greenland would start using U.S. dollars instead of the Danish krone.
* The U.S. would take over Greenland's defense and foreign policy (bye-bye, Denmark).
* Federal agencies (FBI, TSA, EPA, IRS) would begin setting up operations.

- What stays the same?
* Greenland's local government would continue running day-to-day affairs.
* Greenland wouldn't have full voting rights in Congress yet (just like Puerto Rico).

This phase would last anywhere from 5 to 10 years—giving Greenland time to adjust to the American system before full statehood.

Step 3: Greenland Drafts a State Constitution

Just like every other state, Greenland would need a constitution outlining its governance, laws, and relationship with the federal government.

Would Greenland keep its Indigenous identity? – The new constitution would protect Greenlandic culture, language, and traditions while integrating with U.S. law.

Would English become the official language? – Maybe, but Greenlandic (Kalaallisut) could still be an official state language, much like Hawaiian is in Hawaii.

Would Greenland get a governor? – Yep! Greenland would elect a governor and state legislature, just like every other U.S. state.

Drafting this constitution would likely take years of legal discussions, negotiations, and at least one lawyer making a bad pun about icebergs.

Step 4: Greenland Elects Its First U.S. Representatives

Once Greenland graduates from being a U.S. territory, it would gain:
* Two U.S. Senators (because every state gets two, even tiny ones like Wyoming).
* At least one Representative in the House (possibly more, depending on population growth).

Imagine the first Greenlandic senator giving a speech in Congress—most likely starting with:

"Mr. President, I am honored to represent the coldest state in the union. And no, I will not be introducing a bill for unlimited free ice cream... yet."

2. How Long Would the Full Transition Take?

If we look at the history of previous statehood processes (Alaska, Hawaii, and even Puerto Rico's long battle for status), the full transition for Greenland would likely take:

Phase 1: Congressional Approval (1-2 years)
Phase 2: Territorial Period (5-10 years)
Phase 3: Drafting State Constitution (2-5 years)
Phase 4: Full Statehood Approval & Elections (1-2 years)

- Total Estimated Timeline: 10-20 years from referendum to full statehood.

(Translation: If Greenland voted "yes" today, it probably wouldn't be an official state until somewhere between 2035 and 2045.)

That's longer than some people spend paying off student loans!

3. How Would Greenlandic Governance Change?

Once fully integrated as a U.S. state, Greenland would function like every other state—with a few Arctic-specific twists.

* What Stays the Same?
* Greenland would still have a local government, state courts, and control over state laws.

* Greenland could keep its cultural traditions, like Indigenous hunting rights and Greenlandic-language education.

* The U.S. would respect Greenland's autonomy—much like it does with Hawaii's unique cultural status.

* What Changes?

* Greenland would have to follow all U.S. federal laws—meaning more regulations, taxes, and federal agencies.

* Greenland would be directly involved in U.S. elections—with its own presidential primary and Electoral College votes.

* Greenland might see an influx of U.S. businesses and investments—which could change its economy and culture over time.

(McDonald's Nuuk? Starbucks Ilulissat? The possibilities are endless!)

4. Would Greenland Be Happy as a U.S. State?

Even if Greenland successfully became the 51st state, there would still be big questions about how people would adjust.

- Would Greenlanders feel like full Americans—or outsiders?

- Would statehood bring prosperity—or unexpected challenges?

- Would Greenland have second thoughts about joining the union?

History shows that statehood is a long and sometimes bumpy road (ask Hawaii or Alaska), but it also brings opportunities that territories don't have.

At the very least, Greenland would have a seat at the table in Washington, D.C.—and a whole new identity as America's Arctic stronghold.

Final Verdict: What If Greenland Said Yes?

- Statehood would be a long, complex process—likely taking 10-20 years.
- Greenland would gain political representation, economic growth, and federal support.
- U.S. laws, businesses, and infrastructure would reshape Greenland's daily life.
- Cultural and environmental concerns would be ongoing debates—but Greenland would still retain much of its Inuit identity.

Would Greenland be better off as a U.S. state?

That's a question only Greenlanders can answer.

But one thing's for sure—if Greenland ever did join the U.S., it would be the most unique and fascinating state in American history.

(Also, let's be real—nothing would be cooler than seeing an Arctic sled dog on a U.S. license plate.)

CHAPTER

15

COMPARING GREENLAND
TO OTHER U.S. STATES

Comparing Greenland to Other U.S. States
   - Would Greenland be more like Alaska or Hawaii?
 - Taxation, governance, and local autonomy
 - Could Greenland become a state without losing its identity?

If Greenland were to join the United States, it wouldn't just be another state—it would be the most unique state in American history.

Think about it.

* Largest landmass (sorry, Alaska).
* Smallest population (Wyoming finally gets some competition).
* Only state with more sled dogs than cars.
* First state where the phrase "frozen assets" is taken literally.

But what would Greenland actually be like as a state?

Would it resemble Alaska, with its Arctic isolation and re-source wealth?

Would it be like Hawaii, a geographically remote state with a strong Indigenous culture?

Or would Greenland be something entirely different—an American state like no other?

Let's break it down.

1. Would Greenland Be More Like Alaska or Hawaii?

Let's compare Greenland to the two most geographically unique states in the U.S.—Alaska and Hawaii.

Category	Greenland	Alaska	Hawaii
Geography	Arctic tundra, glaciers, fjords	Arctic tundra, forests, mountains	Tropical islands, volcanoes, beaches
Climate	Cold. Always. Seriously.	Cold, but with some warmer summers	Warm. Always. Seriously.
Population	~56,000	~730,000	~1.4 million
Main Industries	Fishing, mining, tourism	Oil, fishing, tourism	Tourism, agriculture, military
Language	Greenlandic, Danish, English	English, Indigenous languages	English, Hawaiian, Pidgin
Transportation	No roads between cities; mostly boats & planes	Roads, rail, air, boats	Roads, air, boats

Similarities to Alaska

- Extreme weather, rugged terrain, and isolated communities.
- Strong reliance on natural resources (fishing, mining, energy).
- Large landmass with a small population.

If Greenland became a U.S. state, it would likely get treated a lot like Alaska, with federal investments in infrastructure, Arctic research, and military presence.

(Imagine the "Alaska Permanent Fund Dividend" but for Greenland—every resident could get an annual check from U.S. oil and mineral revenues!)

Similarities to Hawaii

- Unique Indigenous culture that's distinct from the mainland U.S.
- A long history of self-governance before joining the U.S.
- Potential for tourism growth due to natural beauty and isolation.

Hawaii's Indigenous heritage has remained strong despite statehood, so Greenland could follow a similar path—maintaining its Inuit traditions while integrating into American governance.

(Just don't expect Greenlanders to start playing the ukulele anytime soon.)

2. Taxation, Governance, and Local Autonomy

One of the biggest concerns about Greenland becoming a state would be taxation and governance.

Would Greenland keep its financial independence, or would it have to start paying for things it never had to before?

How Would Taxes Change?

Right now, Greenlanders:
- Pay taxes to the Greenlandic government (not Denmark directly).
- Don't have U.S. federal income tax (because they're not part of the U.S.).

If Greenland became a U.S. state, things would change:
* Federal income tax would apply—meaning Greenlanders would have to file with the IRS (yikes).
* Sales tax, property tax, and state taxes might change depending on Greenland's new policies.
* Greenland could receive billions in federal funding for infrastructure, education, and public services.

Would Greenlanders be okay with paying federal taxes in exchange for state benefits?

(Let's be honest—nobody likes paying taxes, but free public schools and healthcare funding might help soften the blow.)

How Much Autonomy Would Greenland Keep?

Even as a U.S. state, Greenland would likely maintain a lot of local autonomy, similar to:

* Hawaii, which has protected its Indigenous culture, language, and land rights.

* Alaska, which gets special federal funding for its isolated communities.

Could Greenland set its own policies? Yes!

- It could have bilingual laws in Greenlandic and English, like Hawaii does with Hawaiian.

- It could regulate its own hunting and fishing industries to protect Inuit traditions.

- It could elect a state government that represents Greenlandic interests first.

Basically, Greenland wouldn't lose its identity—it would just gain federal support and representation.

(Think of it as an expansion pack for Greenland, not a total system reset.)

3. Could Greenland Become a State Without Losing Its Identity?

One of the biggest fears Greenlanders would have about joining the U.S. is cultural assimilation.

Would statehood mean the slow erasure of Greenlandic traditions, language, and Inuit heritage?

Not necessarily.

How Greenland Could Protect Its Identity as a State

1. Keep Greenlandic as an Official Language – Just like Hawaiian is co-official in Hawaii, Greenland could keep its language policies intact.

2. Indigenous Land & Hunting Rights – Similar to Native American reservations, Greenland could create legal protections for traditional hunting, fishing, and land ownership.

3. Limit Outside Influence – Greenland could regulate foreign business expansion to prevent over-commercialization (ahem, looking at you, Walmart).

4. State-Controlled Tourism Growth – Instead of letting mega-corporations overrun Greenland's natural beauty, the state could develop eco-friendly tourism industries that respect the land.

5. Green Energy Instead of Oil-Dependence – Instead of becoming another Texas or Alaska, Greenland could focus on wind, hydro, and renewable resources—positioning itself as America's greenest state.

(After all, it's literally called GREENland.)

Would Greenland Lose Some Cultural Influence?

Probably—just like Hawaii and Alaska became more "American" over time.

But if Greenland proactively protected its traditions, it could keep its Inuit identity strong while still enjoying the benefits of statehood.

(In other words, it could be the first U.S. state where people celebrate both the Fourth of July and the Arctic Winter Games.)

Final Verdict: What Kind of State Would Greenland Be?

Greenland wouldn't be exactly like Alaska or Hawaii—it would be a hybrid.

Like Alaska, it would be cold, resource-rich, and strategically important.
Like Hawaii, it would have a unique Indigenous culture that sets it apart.
Like neither, it would be the first U.S. state with more sled dogs than cars.

- It could thrive as a U.S. state while keeping its traditions alive.
- It would receive massive federal support, infrastructure funding, and economic opportunities.
- It would add a fascinating new chapter to U.S. history.

Would it still be the same Greenland? No. But would it be a stronger, more developed, and globally influential version of itself?

That's a possibility worth exploring.

INTERNATIONAL BACKLASH

I nternational Backlash – Who Wouldn't Like This?
   - Denmark's reaction
  - China and Russia's Arctic ambitions
  - The impact on NATO and global diplomacy

So, let's say Greenland shocks the world and says "Yes" to becoming the 51st state of the United States.

The U.S. celebrates. Greenland celebrates. Maybe even a few confused Canadians celebrate (they still don't know what to do with their own Arctic territory).

But not everyone would be thrilled. In fact, some countries might throw a diplomatic tantrum big enough to melt an iceberg (which, to be fair, is already happening).

From Denmark feeling betrayed to Russia and China freaking out over U.S. Arctic expansion, Greenlandic statehood could trigger some serious international backlash.

Let's break down who wouldn't like this, why they'd object, and whether the U.S. would need to prepare for some very frosty diplomatic relations.

1. Denmark's Reaction – "Wait... That's OUR Island!"

Denmark has ruled Greenland since 1814, and even though Greenland has broad autonomy, it's still officially part of the Kingdom of Denmark.

So if Greenland suddenly joined the U.S., how would Denmark react?

Scenario 1: Denmark Takes It Like a Cool Viking (Unlikely)
- Denmark could accept the decision, shake hands with the U.S., and move on.
- It could focus on its remaining territories, like the Faroe Islands.
- It could negotiate compensation for losing Greenland (think of it like a geopolitical divorce settlement).

(Reality check: This scenario is about as likely as finding a palm tree in Greenland.)

Scenario 2: Denmark Fights Back (Much More Likely)
Denmark could strongly oppose Greenland's U.S. statehood, leading to:

Legal challenges – Denmark could argue in international courts that Greenland's independence vote was invalid or influenced by the U.S.

Economic retaliation – Denmark might cut financial ties with Greenland, forcing the U.S. to absorb billions in additional costs.

Diplomatic fury – Relations between Denmark and the U.S. could sour, making future NATO and EU negotiations awkward.

Scenario 3: Denmark Goes Full Drama Mode

Denmark could rally the European Union to condemn U.S. expansion, framing it as:

* "American Imperialism in the Arctic"
* "An Illegal Land Grab"
* "The Worst Danish-American Feud Since Someone Put Ketchup on a Hot Dog"

Would Denmark cut ties with the U.S. over Greenland? Probably not—it still needs NATO and economic partnerships.

But would it drag Washington through the diplomatic mud for years?

Absolutely.

(The Danish might be polite, but they don't forget easily—just ask the Vikings.)

2. China and Russia's Arctic Ambitions – "Hey, That's OUR Strategic Playground!"

Now, let's talk about the two biggest geopolitical elephants in the Arctic: Russia and China.

Why Would Russia Care?

If Greenland became part of the U.S., Russia would see it as a direct military threat for a few reasons:

The Arctic is Russia's backyard – Russia has nearly 50% of Arctic coastline, and it's trying to dominate Arctic trade routes and military presence.

Greenland's location is too strategic to ignore – Russia already hates that the U.S. has Thule Air Base in Greenland. If the whole island became a U.S. state, Russia's northern security would be even more compromised.

More NATO influence in the Arctic – Russia sees NATO as a major rival. A U.S.-controlled Greenland would mean even stronger Western control over the Arctic region.

How Would Russia React?
* More military expansion – Expect more Russian Arctic military bases, missile tests, and "training exercises" (which are never just training).
* More aggressive rhetoric – Russia would frame U.S. statehood in Greenland as a Western plot to surround it (which, to be fair, wouldn't be entirely wrong).
* Economic partnerships with anti-U.S. allies – Russia could strengthen ties with China, boosting joint Arctic projects.

(Spoiler alert: If Russia starts sending submarines closer to Greenland, expect a very interesting Pentagon press conference.)

Why Would China Care?

Now, China isn't even an Arctic country, but that hasn't stopped it from calling itself a "Near-Arctic Power" (which is like Mexico calling itself a Near-Canadian Power).

China's Interests in Greenland

Mining & Resources – China has invested in Greenland's rare earth minerals, hoping to secure access before the U.S. or EU do.

Arctic Shipping Routes – A U.S.-controlled Greenland could disrupt China's plans for future trade routes through melting Arctic waters.

Expanding Influence – China sees the Arctic as the next frontier for global power competition, and losing Greenland would be a major setback.

How Would China React?

* Condemn U.S. expansion – Expect strong diplomatic protests from Beijing.

* Push for economic influence elsewhere – China could increase investment in Arctic countries like Canada and Norway as a counterweight.

* Strengthen alliances with Russia – A Greenlandic statehood move could bring China and Russia closer together in Arctic strategy.

(Translation: Expect a LOT of angry press releases from Beijing and Moscow.)

3. Impact on NATO and Global Diplomacy

Greenland's U.S. statehood wouldn't just shake up Denmark, Russia, and China—it would reshape the entire NATO alliance and global Arctic politics.

How Would NATO Be Affected?

More U.S. control in the Arctic – NATO already benefits from Thule Air Base, but a fully U.S.-controlled Greenland would solidify Arctic dominance.

Potential European backlash – Some NATO allies (especially Denmark and maybe France) might resent the U.S. for expanding its influence without European input.

Tensions with Russia – If NATO increases its Arctic military presence, Russia will retaliate with more aggressive policies.

Could the U.N. Get Involved?

If Greenland's statehood triggered global controversy, expect:
U.N. debates over "territorial sovereignty" and whether Greenland was pressured into statehood.
Economic sanctions from rival nations (China and Russia might try to block U.S. Arctic expansion).
Legal challenges in international courts (especially from Denmark).

(Basically, if Greenland joined the U.S., expect the United Nations to host at least five emergency meetings about it.)

Final Verdict: Who Wouldn't Like Greenlandic Statehood?

- Denmark would fight it legally, economically, and diplomatically.
- Russia would see it as a military threat and respond aggressively.
- China would view it as a loss in the Arctic power struggle.

- NATO and the U.N. would face diplomatic chaos.

Would the U.S. still go through with Greenlandic statehood despite the backlash?

That depends on whether Washington thinks the benefits outweigh the inevitable international drama.

(Hint: The U.S. isn't exactly known for avoiding international drama.)

THE ROLE OF THE MEDIA

The Role of the Media – Selling the Idea to the American Public

- How Greenland statehood would be portrayed in the media
- The power of public perception
- Political messaging and public relations

So, let's say Greenland officially votes YES to statehood.

The politicians are excited.
The Pentagon is making new Arctic military plans.
The business world is licking its chops over rare earth minerals and tourism opportunities.

But there's one last hurdle: Convincing the American people that adding a giant, ice-covered island to the U.S. is a good idea.

Because let's be honest—if you walked up to the average American on the street and asked, "Do you think Greenland should be a U.S. state?", the responses would likely include:

"Greenland? Where's that?"

"Isn't it warm there?" (No, that's Iceland. I know, it's confusing.)

"Does it come with free healthcare?" (Um, that's... complicated.)

In a world where public perception shapes policy, how would the U.S. government, politicians, and media sell Greenlandic statehood to the American people?

Would it be pitched as an economic and strategic masterstroke—or would it be turned into a punchline on late-night TV?

Let's explore how Greenland would be marketed, messaged, and meme'd into the American consciousness.

1. How Greenland Statehood Would Be Portrayed in the Media

First things first: What kind of headlines would Greenlandic statehood generate?

Would it be a media sensation like Alaska and Hawaii's statehood bids?

Or would it be treated like a bizarre "what-if" scenario—something fun to debate, but not seriously considered?

The Positive Media Spin: "America Expands Into the Future"

If the U.S. government wanted to promote Greenlandic statehood, the messaging would focus on:

* Economic Prosperity – "Greenland's untapped resources will create jobs and strengthen the U.S. economy!"
* National Security – "Statehood will give the U.S. a strategic Arctic advantage over Russia and China!"
* Cultural Enrichment – "Greenland's Inuit heritage will bring new traditions and diversity to the United States!"
* Adventure & Tourism – "America is getting its own winter wonderland!"

(Picture a dramatic campaign ad: A majestic iceberg, the American flag waving in the Arctic wind, and Morgan Freeman narrating, "This... is the future of the United States.")

The Negative Media Spin: "Another Government Boondoggle?"

On the other hand, not everyone would be on board. The media could frame Greenlandic statehood as:

* A Financial Drain – "Why should American taxpayers foot the bill for an island that's mostly ice?"
* A Military Overreach – "Is the U.S. just using Greenland to provoke Russia?"
* A Cultural Misfit – "Does Greenland even want to be American?"
* Another Puerto Rico Situation – "Will Greenland actually get fair representation in Congress, or will it be ignored?"

(And of course, every late-night host will make at least one joke about Trump trying to build a hotel there.)

2. The Power of Public Perception – What Do Americans Actually Think?

Here's the thing—public opinion matters.

No matter how much politicians love an idea, if the average American isn't on board, it's not going anywhere.

So, what do Americans actually think about Greenland?

Historical U.S. Interest in Greenland

1946 – The U.S. offered to buy Greenland from Denmark for $100 million. Denmark said no.
2019 – President Donald Trump floated the idea of buying Greenland—and the media turned it into a joke.

(Let's be real: If the U.S. had pushed Greenlandic statehood in a more serious way, would Americans have responded differently?)

Current Public Awareness

If you polled the average American today...
- Most wouldn't know much about Greenland (except that it's cold).
- Some would be confused about why the U.S. even wants it.
- A few might think it's already part of Canada. (Spoiler: It's not.)

Would public opinion shift if the media covered Greenland seriously? Absolutely.

Would that coverage be positive, negative, or hilarious? That depends on who controls the narrative.

3. Political Messaging and Public Relations – How to Sell Greenlandic Statehood

If Greenland were on the verge of statehood, how would politicians sell the idea to the American public?

Well, it depends who's talking.

Republican Messaging: "Security, Resources, and Energy Independence"
- "Greenland is a natural extension of Alaska—think of it as Alaska's little cousin!"
- "This strengthens America's control over Arctic trade routes!"
- "Let's develop Greenland's energy resources and become less dependent on foreign oil!"

(Fun fact: If Greenland had a lot of oil, the "Drill, Baby, Drill" slogan would be making a comeback in campaign speeches.)

Democratic Messaging: "Climate Change, Indigenous Rights, and Green Energy"
- "We will protect Greenland's environment while investing in green technology!"
- "Statehood gives Greenlanders full rights and representation in the U.S.!"
- "A sustainable Arctic future begins with integrating Greenland into a green economy!"

(Picture an ad with wind turbines on Greenland's icy land-scape, featuring hopeful music and someone saying, "The future is now.")

Social Media and Meme Culture: "Make Greenland Cool Again"

No modern political movement succeeds without meme power.

Imagine Twitter, TikTok, and Reddit during the Greenlandic statehood debate:

Twitter:
"Greenland should be a state. Change my mind."
"Can't wait for the Greenland vs. Alabama college football matchup."
"Space Force... but in the Arctic. LET'S GOOOO."

TikTok:
A viral dance to "Cold as Ice" by Foreigner, celebrating Greenlandic statehood.
A challenge where people try to "survive" Greenland's winter in shorts and flip-flops.
Someone racing a sled dog team while wearing an American flag cape.

Reddit Debates:
"Would Greenland be a red state or a blue state?"
"Would Greenland's time zones finally fix daylight saving time?"
"What happens if you leave a McDonald's burger outside in Greenland for a year?"

(The answer: It probably wouldn't decompose, because... well, it's frozen.)

Final Verdict: Can the Media Sell Greenlandic Statehood?

- If framed positively, the American public could be convinced that Greenland is an economic and strategic win.
- If mishandled, it could become another divisive political issue that gets stuck in endless debate.
- Social media would have a FIELD DAY, whether it's serious or just a meme-fest.

Would Greenlandic statehood win over the hearts and minds of Americans?

It all depends on the story that gets told.

(And let's be honest, if America can sell pineapple on pizza, it can probably sell Greenland as a state.)

IS STATEHOOD THE BEST OPTION?

Is Statehood the Best Option? Exploring Other Models
   - U.S. territories: Puerto Rico and Guam comparisons
 - Free association agreements
 - Economic and military partnerships without full statehood

After all the heated debates, global backlash, and meme-worthy news cycles, it's time to ask:

 - Is full statehood really the best option for Greenland?

Sure, becoming the 51st state would come with federal funding, economic development, and a sweet new addition to the American flag.

But what if there's a middle ground—a way for Greenland to get the benefits of U.S. partnership without fully giving up its autonomy?

Before we start sewing new stars onto the flag, let's explore other political models that might work better—from U.S. territories to free association agreements and strategic partnerships.

Because sometimes the best solution isn't a wedding—it's just moving in together.

1. U.S. Territories: Puerto Rico and Guam Comparisons

If Greenland doesn't want full statehood, but still wants a strong U.S. connection, it could become a U.S. territory—just like Puerto Rico, Guam, and the U.S. Virgin Islands.

What's a U.S. Territory, Anyway?

A U.S. territory is part of the United States but... also not fully part of it (yes, it's confusing).

* Residents are U.S. nationals (but sometimes not full citizens).
* Territories have local governments but are subject to U.S. federal law.
* They don't get full voting representation in Congress (no senators, limited House reps).

Would This Work for Greenland?

- Yes, because:
- Greenland would keep its autonomy while enjoying economic and security benefits.
- It wouldn't have to pay U.S. federal income tax (which Greenlanders would probably love).

- It could receive federal aid and investment without fully giving up its identity.

* No, because:
- Greenlanders wouldn't get full voting rights in Congress.
- The U.S. would still have a lot of influence over Greenland's policies.
- Greenland might end up stuck in political limbo—like Puerto Rico, which has debated statehood for decades.

Verdict:
Becoming a U.S. territory would be a compromise option—giving Greenland many U.S. benefits without fully committing to statehood.

(Think of it as dating instead of getting married—less paperwork, fewer in-laws.)

2. Free Association Agreements – The Best of Both Worlds?

Greenland could also follow the "Free Association" model—a special political relationship where it remains independent but partners closely with the U.S.

What is Free Association?

A Free Association agreement is like saying:
- "We're independent, but let's stay close friends."
- "You can handle my military defense, but I'll make my own domestic policies."
- "Let's work together, but I'm still my own country."

Who Has This Setup?

The Marshall Islands, Palau, and Micronesia all have Free Association Agreements with the U.S..

- They are sovereign nations, but the U.S. provides military protection, economic aid, and free movement of citizens.

- Their citizens can live and work in the U.S., but they don't vote in U.S. elections.

Would This Work for Greenland?

- Yes, because:

- Greenland would stay independent but maintain U.S. protection and financial aid.

- It could still develop its own trade policies without U.S. interference.

- Greenlanders could get access to U.S. citizenship benefits without full integration.

* No, because:

- The U.S. would still expect military bases and geopolitical influence.

- Greenland might feel like it's not fully in control of its own future.

- Denmark might oppose this model since it would shift Greenland even further from its orbit.

Verdict:

A Free Association agreement would allow Greenland to stay independent while still benefiting from U.S. support—making it a strong alternative to statehood.

(It's like getting all the perks of a gym membership without signing a long-term contract.)

3. Economic and Military Partnerships Without Full State-hood

If Greenland wants to keep its independence but still benefit from U.S. economic and military ties, it could explore a strategic partnership model—like many countries do today.

Option 1: Military Partnership

More U.S. military presence – Greenland could allow the U.S. to expand Thule Air Base in exchange for defense funding and security guarantees.

Military investment – The U.S. could fund coastal security, Arctic surveillance, and emergency response infrastructure in Greenland.

Joint Arctic strategy – Greenland could work with the U.S. on climate change, Arctic trade routes, and regional defense.

(Think of this as the U.S. offering Greenland a "Platinum Defense Membership" card.)

Option 2: Economic Partnership

Energy and Mining Investments – U.S. companies could invest in Greenland's rare earth minerals, green energy, and fisheries—boosting the local economy.

Trade Deals – Greenland could negotiate special trade agreements with the U.S. to expand its exports.

Tourism Development – The U.S. could help fund sustainable tourism, making Greenland a major Arctic travel destination.

(Because nothing says "Welcome to America" like a cruise ship docking in Nuuk.)

Verdict:

A partnership model would let Greenland keep full independence while still benefiting from U.S. support—a more flexible and low-commitment approach than statehood.

(It's like saying, "Let's be business partners, not roommates.")

Final Verdict: What's the Best Option for Greenland?

So, after exploring every possible model, what's the best path forward for Greenland?

- Statehood?
- Pros: Full U.S. funding, voting rights, economic growth.
- Cons: Loss of independence, cultural risks, major geopolitical drama.
- Final Thought: Great for U.S. strategy, but might be too extreme for Greenlanders.

- U.S. Territory?
- Pros: Economic support without full assimilation.
- Cons: No full political representation, potential economic reliance.
- Final Thought: A middle ground, but still ties Greenland closely to Washington.

- Free Association?
- Pros: Greenland stays independent but gets U.S. protection and economic aid.
- Cons: Less global recognition, Denmark might oppose it.

- Final Thought: A great balance of autonomy and support.

- Strategic Partnerships?
- Pros: Full independence with U.S. military and economic benefits.
- Cons: No official U.S. citizenship for Greenlanders, less political integration.
- Final Thought: Probably the easiest and least controversial option.

So, should Greenland become the 51st state?

- Maybe not yet. But closer U.S.-Greenland relations—through economic, military, or Free Association agreements—could be the next step.

Would full statehood happen eventually?

That depends on how history unfolds—and whether Greenland ever decides that the stars and stripes suit it better than the Danish crown.

(For now, the biggest debate should probably be: "How do we convince Americans to actually learn where Greenland is on a map?")

GREENLAND'S IMPACT ON U.S. ELECTIONS

G reenland's Impact on U.S. Elections
 - Electoral college changes
 - Would Greenland vote Republican or Democrat?
 - How political parties might strategize

So, after all the legal battles, geopolitical drama, and media spin, Greenland becomes the 51st state of the United States.

The ink is barely dry on the statehood paperwork when a new political question emerges:

 - How will Greenland affect U.S. elections?

Would it tilt the balance of power toward Democrats or Republicans?

Would political strategists start campaigning on dog sleds and debating in igloos?

Would Greenland finally be the state that ends the Electoral College? (Okay, probably not, but a professor can dream...)

Let's break it all down—electoral votes, party politics, and how Greenland could shake up the American political landscape.

1. How Would the Electoral College Change?

First, let's address the biggest change Greenland's statehood would bring to U.S. elections—more electoral votes.

How the Electoral College Works (In Case You Forgot Civics Class)
- Each state gets electoral votes based on its population (number of House representatives + 2 senators).
- Currently, there are 538 electoral votes—270 needed to win the presidency.
- Adding a new state means adding new electoral votes, potentially shifting the balance of power.

How Many Electoral Votes Would Greenland Get?

Let's compare with other small-population states:

State	Population	Electoral Votes
Wyoming	~580,000	3
Vermont	~650,000	3
Alaska	~730,000	3
Greenland	~56,000	???

Under the minimum rules of the Electoral College, Greenland would automatically get:

- 1 House representative (based on its population, even though it's small).
- 2 Senators (because every state gets two).

Total Electoral Votes for Greenland: 3

(Which, hilariously, means Greenland would have the same presidential election influence as Wyoming, despite having 90% fewer people.)

So, while Greenland wouldn't be a game-changer in presidential elections, it would matter in tight races (looking at you, Florida).

2. Would Greenland Vote Republican or Democrat?

Now, here's the fun part—which party would Greenland support?

Political Leanings of Greenland

* Social Welfare – Greenland has a strong social safety net, relying heavily on government funding and services—which aligns more with Democratic policies.
* Environmental Concerns – Climate change is a huge issue for Greenland, meaning pro-environment policies (usually Democratic) would be popular.
* Indigenous Rights – Greenland has a large Inuit population that values autonomy and cultural preservation, often supported by progressive policies.

But Could Republicans Win Greenland?

Possibly, if they focused on:

* Economic Growth & Energy Development – If Republicans pitched resource extraction (mining, oil, etc.) as a job creator, some Greenlanders might support it.

* Strong Military & Arctic Defense – Greenlanders value security, and Republican-led defense policies might appeal to them.

Final Answer? Likely Democratic-leaning, but Competitive

Most experts would predict Greenland as a "safe blue" state, much like Hawaii or Vermont.

But with the right economic arguments, Republicans could compete (especially if Greenland's economy shifts toward private sector jobs).

(Translation: Greenland would be the state that Democrats assume they'll win, but Republicans would try to flip every few election cycles—especially if mining jobs are on the ballot.)

3. How Political Parties Might Strategize Greenland's Vote

Once Greenland becomes a state, political parties will immediately start strategizing on how to win its votes.

How Democrats Would Campaign in Greenland

Key Messages:
- "We will protect Greenland's environment and fight climate change."
- "We will increase federal funding for infrastructure and jobs."
- "We will ensure Greenlanders have equal rights and representation."

Winning Strategy:

- Emphasize climate policy, Indigenous rights, and federal investment.

- Highlight Greenland's existing social programs to show alignment with progressive policies.

- Send popular Democratic figures (maybe Barack Obama?) to campaign in Nuuk.

(Imagine the campaign slogan: "A Brighter Future for Greenland—Still Cold, but Brighter.")

How Republicans Would Campaign in Greenland

Key Messages:

- "Greenland's resources should benefit Greenlanders—let's develop industries and create jobs!"

- "Stronger national security in the Arctic will protect Greenland and America."

- "You don't want Washington, D.C., controlling your lives—vote for independence-minded leadership."

Winning Strategy:

- Focus on economic development, especially in mining, energy, and tourism.

- Target Greenland's business community with pro-growth, lower-tax policies.

- Frame Democrats as too bureaucratic, arguing that Greenlanders should keep more of their earnings.

(Imagine the campaign ad: "Jobs. Security. Freedom. Let's Put Greenland First.")

Would Greenland Be a Swing State?

Probably not at first, but in close elections, every electoral vote matters.

In an election where 270 electoral votes are needed to win, Greenland's 3 votes could be the deciding factor in a razor-thin race.

(Imagine a future where candidates have to stop in Nuuk for campaign rallies—what a world!)

Final Verdict: Would Greenland Matter in U.S. Elections?

- It would add 3 electoral votes, which could be decisive in close elections.
- It would likely lean Democratic, but Republicans could compete with economic arguments.
- Both parties would start campaigning in Greenland, bringing U.S. elections to the Arctic for the first time.

Would Greenland single-handedly decide presidential elections?

No. But would it shake things up and force politicians to care about Arctic issues?

Absolutely.

(And let's be honest—who wouldn't want to see a presidential debate held in an igloo?)

WHAT'S IN IT FOR THE GREENLANDERS?

What's in It for the Greenlanders?
 - Social programs, infrastructure, and development
- The cost of U.S. citizenship for Greenlanders
- Balancing self-determination with economic security

So far, we've looked at how the U.S. would benefit from Greenlandic statehood—more military presence, economic opportunities, and bragging rights over Russia and China.

But what about the 56,000 actual people living in Greenland?

- Would statehood make life better for Greenlanders, or would they regret trading Denmark's cozy Nordic welfare system for the bureaucracy of Washington, D.C.?

Would U.S. citizenship be a golden ticket or a headache? And could Greenland balance self-determination with economic security under the American flag?

Let's break it all down—the perks, the price, and the politics of what statehood would mean for the everyday Greenlander.

1. The Good Stuff: Social Programs, Infrastructure, and Development

Let's start with the perks of statehood—because if you're going to join a country, you should at least get something out of it.

* U.S. Federal Funding = More Roads, Schools, and Hospitals
Right now, Greenland relies on Denmark for nearly half its budget—but under U.S. statehood, it would receive:

- Billions in federal infrastructure funding – Roads, bridges, harbors, and airports (finally, no more snowmobile commutes).
- Investment in public services – More hospitals, better schools, improved utilities.
- More jobs from government projects – Construction, transportation, and federal agency jobs would create new employment opportunities.

(Translation: Fewer potholes, faster WiFi, and maybe even a Starbucks or two.)

* More Economic Opportunities

Access to U.S. Business & Trade Networks – Greenlandic companies would be able to sell products freely across all 50 states.

Bigger Tourism Industry – As an official U.S. state, Greenland would see more cruise ships, adventure tourists, and eco-travelers (just hopefully not spring breakers).

More Private Investment – U.S. companies might expand mining, energy, and fisheries industries, boosting Greenland's economy.

(Think of it as Greenland getting a VIP pass to the world's biggest economy.)

* Better Education and Healthcare Access

Greenlanders would be eligible for U.S. federal student aid – making college more affordable.

More healthcare options – With U.S. citizenship, Greenlanders could access Medicare, Medicaid, and American hospitals.

Would these programs completely replace Denmark's strong welfare system? No, but they'd offer new opportunities that don't exist under Danish rule.

(At the very least, Greenlanders would finally get access to U.S. Netflix without using a VPN.)

2. The Trade-Offs: The Cost of U.S. Citizenship for Greenlanders

Now, let's talk about the price of statehood—because nothing in life (or politics) is free.

* Taxes, Taxes, Taxes

Right now, Greenlanders don't pay U.S. federal income tax. But under statehood, they'd have to file with the IRS every April 15th like every other American.

New taxes Greenlanders would face:
- Federal income tax (no more Denmark subsidies—Washington needs its cut).
- U.S. sales tax and property taxes (depending on Greenland's state laws).
- Social Security & Medicare payroll taxes (so they can retire in Florida like a true American).

(If you thought Greenland was cold, wait until someone sees their first IRS bill.)

* Cultural Concerns – Would Greenland Lose Its Identity?

Greenlandic (Kalaallisut) vs. English – Would Greenland be forced to switch to English for official business?

Protecting Indigenous Traditions – Could Greenland maintain its Inuit heritage under American governance?

Traditional Hunting vs. U.S. Wildlife Laws – Would federal environmental regulations clash with Greenland's centuries-old hunting practices?

(Fun fact: Greenlanders hunt seals, which could spark debates over animal rights—imagine that Senate hearing.)

* More Bureaucracy and Federal Control

More U.S. Government Oversight – Greenland would have to follow U.S. laws on everything from banking regulations to energy policy.

Dealing with Washington, D.C. – Greenlanders would have two senators and at least one representative, but would they have real influence in Congress?

(Let's be honest—getting Congress to pay attention to Alaska is already tough. Greenland would be like Alaska's even frostier cousin.)

3. Balancing Self-Determination with Economic Security

This is the real question—does Greenland want to trade some independence for long-term economic security?

The Case for Self-Determination

* Full independence gives Greenland 100% control over its future—no outside influence.
* It could still build its economy through global trade, eco-tourism, and strategic partnerships.
* It wouldn't have to answer to Washington, D.C., Denmark, or anyone else.

(Imagine Greenland as the Switzerland of the Arctic—neutral, independent, and just cold all the time.)

The Case for Economic Security

* Joining the U.S. brings massive financial stability—no worrying about GDP swings.
* Statehood gives Greenland a safety net in uncertain global times.
* It would become part of the most powerful economy and military in the world.

(It's like getting adopted by a rich uncle—sure, you have to follow some house rules, but at least you're not struggling to pay rent.)

Final Verdict: Is Statehood Worth It for Greenlanders?

- Pros of Statehood: More money, more opportunities, better infrastructure, U.S. citizenship.
* Cons of Statehood: Higher taxes, cultural risks, more bureaucracy.

Would Greenlanders vote for statehood today? Probably not yet.

But if Denmark ever stopped providing financial support, Greenland might take another look at the U.S. as a long-term solution.

For now, the best path forward might be a closer U.S.-Greenland relationship without full statehood.

(Because sometimes, it's better to stay friends than rush into marriage.)

THE LEGAL FRAMEWORK

The Legal Framework – Can the Constitution Handle This?
   - Legal barriers to Greenlandic statehood
 - Constitutional amendments and historical precedents
 - Would the Supreme Court get involved?

So, Greenland decides it wants in. The people vote, the politicians agree, and somewhere in Washington, a graphic designer starts mocking up a 51-star American flag (which is going to drive OCD people nuts).

But before we start installing Walmarts in Nuuk, there's a little problem—the U.S. Constitution.

- Can America even legally add Greenland as a state?

Would Congress have the power to approve it?
Would the Supreme Court need to weigh in?

Would we need to rewrite parts of the Constitution (or just pretend it all makes sense, as usual)?

Let's break down the legal barriers, historical precedents, and the constitutional fine print—before the lawyers take over.

1. Legal Barriers to Greenlandic Statehood

Article IV, Section 3 of the U.S. Constitution:
"New States may be admitted by the Congress into this Union..."

Translation: Yes, Congress can add new states—no constitutional amendment required.

This means that legally, Greenland can become a state—as long as Congress and Greenland agree.

(So no, we don't need to dig up the Founding Fathers to get their approval—though I'd love to see Ben Franklin's take on Arctic expansion.)

But... there are still major legal hurdles to overcome.

Hurdle 1: Denmark's Approval (or Lack of It)

Right now, Greenland is an autonomous territory of Denmark, which means:

* Greenland has self-rule in most areas.
* Denmark still controls foreign policy, defense, and big economic decisions.

For Greenland to join the U.S., one of two things must happen:

1. Denmark must agree to transfer Greenland to the U.S. (which seems highly unlikely).

2. Greenland must declare full independence first, then negotiate U.S. statehood separately.

(Translation: Greenland can't just ghost Denmark and run off to Vegas with America—there's paperwork involved.)

Hurdle 2: U.S. Congress Needs to Approve It

For Greenland to become a state, it must pass a vote in both chambers of Congress:

- House of Representatives – Needs a simple majority vote.
- Senate – Also needs a simple majority vote.

This shouldn't be too hard, right?

(Narrator voice: It would, in fact, be very hard.)

Hurdle 3: Would Partisan Politics Block Greenland's Statehood?

Here's the political reality:

- If Greenland is expected to vote Democrat, Republicans might block its statehood.
- If Greenland is expected to vote Republican, Democrats might block it.
- If Greenland is expected to vote for whoever promises more free WiFi, things get interesting.

Just look at Puerto Rico, which has been debating statehood for decades—mostly because U.S. politicians can't agree on whether adding a new state would help or hurt their party.

(So, Greenland might have to wait in line behind Puerto Rico, Washington D.C., and possibly the Moon.)

2. Constitutional Amendments and Historical Precedents

Has the U.S. ever added a state like this before?

Short answer: Sort of.

The Louisiana Purchase (1803) – The U.S. Bought a Giant Landmass
- The U.S. bought Louisiana from France for $15 million.
- There was no clear constitutional rule for buying foreign land... so the U.S. just did it anyway.
- Eventually, Louisiana and several other states formed out of the purchase.

Lesson for Greenland: If America really wants land, it finds a way to make it legal later.

The Alaska Purchase (1867) – Buying a Frozen Landmass Worked Before
- The U.S. bought Alaska from Russia for $7.2 million.
- People at the time mocked the deal, calling it "Seward's Folly" (because who would want a giant, frozen wasteland?).
- Alaska became a full state in 1959—proving that a remote Arctic territory CAN eventually become a U.S. state.

Lesson for Greenland: People laughed at Alaska's statehood... until it became one of the richest resource states in America.

(Imagine "Seward's Folly 2.0," but this time, it's "Biden's Iceberg.")

Hawaii (1959) – An Independent Nation Becomes a State
- Hawaii was an independent kingdom before being annexed by the U.S. in 1898.
- It officially became a state in 1959, after a referendum vote in favor of statehood.

Lesson for Greenland: If Greenland declared independence first, it could later hold a vote to join the U.S.—just like Hawaii did.

(Although, let's be honest, Greenland's tourism slogan won't be as catchy as "The Aloha State.")

3. Would the Supreme Court Get Involved?

If Greenland's statehood became politically messy, could the Supreme Court step in?

Possibly.

Potential Legal Challenges

Denmark Could Sue – If Denmark felt the U.S. was interfering in its affairs, it could take the case to the International Court of Justice (but the U.S. would probably ignore it).

Greenlanders Could Sue for Sovereignty Rights – If Greenlanders felt rushed into statehood, they could challenge the process in court.

Congressional Lawsuits Over Political Balance – If one party felt Greenland's statehood unfairly benefited the other, they might sue to block it.

Verdict: The Supreme Court could get involved, but only if Greenlanders, Denmark, or U.S. politicians challenged the process.

(Otherwise, the justices will probably just sit back and watch the drama unfold like the rest of us.)

Final Verdict: Can the Constitution Handle Greenland's Statehood?

- Legally Possible? Yes.
- Needs a Constitutional Amendment? No.
* Politically Easy? Not at all.

Adding Greenland as the 51st state would be a legal challenge, a political fight, and a geopolitical headache—but it's not impossible.

Would it take years of congressional debate, Supreme Court cases, and international diplomacy?

Absolutely.

Would it be hilarious to see presidential candidates campaigning in parkas and sled dog races?

Also absolutely.

HOW WOULD OTHER
COUNTRIES REACT?

H ow Would Other Countries React?
     - NATO's response
   - Russia and China's strategic interests
   - The global precedent set by Greenland's statehood

So, Greenland has officially joined the United States as the 51st state.

Americans are celebrating, Greenlanders are wondering why there are suddenly so many McDonald's, and the Pentagon is probably already expanding Thule Air Base.

But outside of the U.S., the world is watching in shock.

   - How would NATO react?
   - Would Russia and China see this as a threat?

- And does Greenland's statehood set a global precedent for other countries to follow?

Let's break it all down—the diplomatic side-eye, the military posturing, and whether the world would treat this as a bold move or an act of geopolitical chaos.

1. NATO's Response – A Win for the Alliance or a Political Nightmare?

First, let's talk about NATO, the North Atlantic Treaty Organization—which includes both the U.S. and Denmark (awkward).

Would NATO Support Greenland's Statehood?

* Yes, because...
- The U.S. is already a NATO member, so Greenland would still be part of NATO's defense network—just under U.S. control instead of Denmark.
- A U.S.-controlled Greenland strengthens NATO's Arctic presence, making it harder for Russia to expand in the region.

* No, because...
- Denmark would be furious. Losing Greenland to the U.S. could strain relations within NATO.
- Other small NATO countries might fear U.S. expansionism, worrying that America is setting a dangerous precedent.
- The EU might see it as an American land grab, making future NATO-EU cooperation more difficult.

Final Verdict: NATO would probably accept Greenland's new status—but not without heated diplomatic meetings, passive-aggressive press conferences, and a very awkward NATO summit.

(Expect Denmark to "accidentally" ignore the U.S. ambassador's handshake for a few months.)

2. Russia and China's Strategic Interests – The Arctic Power Struggle Intensifies

Now, let's move to the two superpowers who definitely wouldn't like Greenland joining the U.S.—Russia and China.

Russia's Reaction – "America Just Took Our Arctic Rivalry to the Next Level"

Russia has the longest Arctic coastline in the world and has spent years militarizing the region. It sees the Arctic as a key battleground for future global dominance.

Why Would Russia Hate U.S. Control Over Greenland?

Greenland gives the U.S. more Arctic military power – With full statehood, the U.S. could expand its bases, missile defense systems, and surveillance.

Russia's Northern Fleet would face more U.S. monitoring – Right now, Russia moves its nuclear submarines through Arctic waters. A U.S.-controlled Greenland would make that harder.

It shifts Arctic trade power toward the West – Russia wants to dominate Arctic shipping routes. A stronger U.S. presence in Greenland would challenge that goal.

How Would Russia Respond?

* Increase Arctic military exercises – Expect more Russian warships, more submarine patrols, and more "totally-not-suspicious" Arctic drills.

* Strengthen Arctic alliances – Russia might deepen ties with China, India, and other non-NATO countries to counterbalance U.S. expansion.

* Spread anti-U.S. propaganda – Russian media would likely frame Greenland's statehood as a "hostile takeover", painting America as an imperialist power.

(Expect a Russian news anchor dramatically saying, "First Alaska... now Greenland... what's next, the North Pole?")

China's Reaction – "There Goes Our Arctic Influence"

China isn't an Arctic country (geographically speaking), but it has big Arctic ambitions—calling itself a "Near-Arctic State" (which is like Florida calling itself "Near-Canada").

Why Would China Oppose Greenlandic Statehood?

China has economic interests in Greenland – Beijing has invested in Greenland's rare earth minerals, hoping to secure a key supply chain for electronics and military tech.

A U.S.-controlled Greenland limits China's Arctic expansion – China has been slowly trying to increase its presence in the Arctic—U.S. statehood throws a massive roadblock in that plan.

China wants Arctic shipping control – As the Arctic ice melts, new global trade routes are opening up. China wants to control them—but a U.S.-dominated Greenland would make that harder.

How Would China Respond?

* Condemn the U.S. diplomatically – China might denounce Greenland's statehood at the United Nations, calling it "Western imperialism."

* Increase investments in other Arctic nations – Expect China to ramp up economic partnerships with Canada, Norway, and Russia to counterbalance the U.S.

* Push Arctic trade alliances – China could try to build new Arctic trade routes with Russia, cutting the U.S. out.

(Basically, China would treat Greenlandic statehood like a really bad breakup—with dramatic speeches and a few "you'll regret this" moments.)

3. The Global Precedent: Would Other Countries Follow?

If Greenland became the 51st state, it would set a massive international precedent.

Would other territories suddenly want to join the U.S.?

Would this encourage more separatist movements worldwide?

Or would it make the U.S. look like a 21st-century empire builder?

Let's explore the global ripple effect.

Puerto Rico – "Hey, What About Us?"

If Greenland became a U.S. state, Puerto Rico would demand answers.

- Puerto Rico has held multiple referendums on statehood, with some votes in favor.
- But Congress has stalled the process, leaving Puerto Rico in political limbo.

If Greenland gets fast-tracked to statehood, expect Puerto Rico to say: "Seriously? We've been waiting for decades!"

(At the very least, Greenland statehood would force the U.S. to finally have the Puerto Rico conversation.)

Canada's Arctic Territories – "Should We Join Too?"

If Greenland joins the U.S., would Canada's Arctic regions start thinking about switching teams?

- Canada's Nunavut and Northwest Territories face similar economic and infrastructure challenges as Greenland.
- If Greenland thrives as a U.S. state, some Canadian Arctic communities might wonder if they'd be better off under Washington instead of Ottawa.

(Imagine the chaos if a chunk of Canada suddenly said, "We'd like to be States 52 and 53.")

The Falkland Islands – "Can We Join the U.S. Instead?"

- The Falkland Islands, a British overseas territory, have debated their future for decades.

- If Greenland's U.S. statehood is a success, some in the Falklands might wonder if aligning with the U.S. is a better long-term bet than staying with the UK.

(Because let's face it—if you're choosing between American funding and British austerity, the choice isn't that hard.)

Final Verdict: How Would the World React?

- NATO would accept it—but Denmark would hold a grudge.
- Russia would ramp up Arctic militarization in response.
- China would call it imperialism and look for other Arctic deals.
- Puerto Rico, Canada's Arctic, and other territories might rethink their future.

Would Greenlandic statehood be a peaceful diplomatic process?

* No, it would be a global political firestorm.

Would it reshape Arctic power politics forever?

* Absolutely.

(And let's be honest—the world's first U.S. presidential debate in Greenland would be amazing.)

U.S. STATEHOOD VS. EU
MEMBERSHIP

U.S. Statehood vs. EU Membership – Which Is Better for Greenland?
- Comparing Greenland's options
- Economic and political consequences
- Would Greenlanders prefer closer ties to the EU instead?

At this point, Greenland is at a crossroads.

On one hand, there's U.S. statehood—access to America's massive economy, federal funding, and... well, a lot of American tourists looking for the world's most extreme winter vacation.

On the other hand, there's the European Union—a familiar, nearby political and economic powerhouse that Greenland used to be a part of before it left in 1985 (Brexit before Brexit).

- Would Greenlanders rather rejoin the EU than become the 51st state?

- Which option provides the best economic and political future?

- And, most importantly, which one comes with better snacks—Danish pastries or deep-fried everything?

Let's compare Greenland's options, weigh the economic and political consequences, and see whether Greenland should look West to Washington or East to Brussels.

1. A Brief History of Greenland and the EU

Believe it or not, Greenland was once part of the European Economic Community (EEC)—which later became the European Union (EU).

Why Did Greenland Leave the EU in 1985?

1. Fishing Disputes – The EU wanted access to Greenland's rich fishing waters, but Greenland wanted to protect its own industry.

2. Cultural & Political Mismatch – Greenlanders felt like a tiny colony inside a giant European system.

3. Desire for More Autonomy – Greenland voted 52% in favor of leaving—becoming the first and only territory to exit the EU (way before the UK made it trendy).

(Translation: Greenland broke up with the EU over fishing rights. Imagine if America left NATO because of a barbecue sauce dispute—same energy.)

But could Greenland come back if the benefits were right?

2. Comparing the Benefits: U.S. Statehood vs. EU Membership

Let's compare Greenland's two paths in terms of economics, governance, and political consequences.

Category	U.S. Statehood	EU Membership
Economic Support	Billions in U.S. federal funding for infrastructure and development.	EU economic aid and investment, but Greenland must follow EU regulations.
Fishing Industry	Greenland controls its own fishing policies.	The EU would regulate Greenland's fishing industry, possibly leading to disputes again.
Military & Security	Full U.S. military protection (Greenland = part of NATO).	Still protected through Denmark and NATO, but no U.S. bases.
Political Influence	Greenland gets two U.S. Senators and at least one House Rep.	Greenland would only be a small EU territory—no real political influence.
Trade & Economy	Free trade with all 50 U.S. states and access to American markets.	Access to the EU's single market (450 million consumers).
Culture & Identity	Risk of losing Greenlandic cultural autonomy due to U.S. influence.	Could maintain more independence, but EU rules might still be restrictive.
Bureaucracy Level	Lots of new U.S. laws and regulations to follow.	Even more EU regulations to follow.

(Spoiler: Either option means a LOT of paperwork.)

3. Economic and Political Consequences for Greenland

Now, let's get serious (well, as serious as we can while discussing Arctic geopolitics with a dad joke sense of humor).

Economic Impact: Who Pays More? Who Gains More?

- The U.S. would provide more direct federal funding than the EU, but...
- The EU would give Greenland access to a massive trade network.
- Greenland's fishing industry would be safer under U.S. statehood than in the EU (because Brussels has a long history of overregulating fisheries).

Verdict: If Greenland wants financial stability, the U.S. is the safer bet. If it wants economic independence, the EU is the better option.

Political Consequences: Who Has More Control Over Greenland?

- As a U.S. state, Greenland would get representation in Congress but would have to follow federal laws.
- As an EU member, Greenland would have less political influence (since it would be a small fish in a big pond).
- Greenland could try to negotiate "special status" within the EU, like the Faroe Islands, but that's not guaranteed.

Verdict: If Greenland wants control over its own affairs, neither option is perfect—but U.S. statehood offers more direct representation.

International Relations: How Would the World React?

- If Greenland joins the U.S., Russia and China will see it as an aggressive move by Washington (as we covered in Chapter 22).

- If Greenland joins the EU, the U.S. might feel left out of Arctic affairs, and Denmark would probably feel relieved to keep it in the European family.

- NATO would prefer U.S. statehood, while the UN might favor EU membership (because let's face it, the UN doesn't love when the U.S. expands).

Verdict: Greenland's global allies would change depending on its decision—statehood would make it part of America's military empire, while EU membership would keep it a regional player in European politics.

4. Would Greenlanders Prefer Closer Ties to the EU Instead?

The biggest question isn't what Washington or Brussels wants—it's what the people of Greenland want.

Do Greenlanders Actually Want U.S. Statehood?

Right now, Greenlanders:
See themselves as distinct from both Denmark and the U.S.
Want more autonomy, not less.
Aren't sure if they'd rather be "Greenlandic first" or part of a bigger system.

A 2016 survey showed that 64% of Greenlanders favor full independence from Denmark—but that doesn't mean they want to join the U.S. instead.

(Translation: Greenlanders might want to "live alone" rather than move in with a bigger roommate.)

Would Greenlanders Prefer Rejoining the EU?

Possibly.

* The EU could offer a balance of economic support without full assimilation.
* It would allow Greenland to stay connected to Denmark and Europe while still gaining financial backing.
* If Greenland could negotiate special status, it might get the benefits of EU membership without giving up too much sovereignty.

(Think of it as being "Facebook official" with the EU, rather than getting married to the U.S.)

Final Verdict: U.S. Statehood vs. EU Membership – Which is Better?

- If Greenland wants stability, federal funding, and political influence, the U.S. is the best choice.
- If Greenland wants trade opportunities, cultural autonomy, and a European future, the EU is the safer option.
- If Greenland wants to stay independent, it should continue building its own economy before making any decision.

So...

- Would Greenland vote to join the U.S. today? Probably not.
- Would it rejoin the EU instead? Maybe, if the terms were right.
- Should Greenland keep its options open and play both sides for the best deal? Absolutely.

(Because if you're the most wanted territory in the Arctic, you might as well see who gives the best offer.)

LESSONS FROM ALASKA
AND HAWAII

L essons from Alaska and Hawaii
   - What worked and what didn't when these states joined
   - Differences in geography, culture, and economy
   - Applying these lessons to Greenland

If Greenland ever decided to become the 51st state, it wouldn't be the first time America added a geographically remote, culturally unique, and resource-rich territory to the Union.

- Enter Alaska and Hawaii—the last two states to join the U.S.

Both were non-contiguous, had distinct Indigenous populations, and were seen as "strategic acquisitions" at the time. Sound familiar?

But while Alaska and Hawaii became success stories, their transitions to statehood weren't exactly smooth sailing (or smooth dog-sledding, in Alaska's case).

- What lessons can Greenland learn from them?
- What worked, what didn't, and how does Greenland compare?
- And most importantly, would Greenland also get a state quarter with a polar bear on it?

Let's explore the historical parallels, key challenges, and potential takeaways for Greenland's statehood journey.

1. A Quick History: How Alaska and Hawaii Became States

Alaska (purchased from Russia in 1867) and Hawaii (annexed by the U.S. in 1898) both had long roads to statehood.

Alaska's Journey to Statehood (1959)

- Bought from Russia for $7.2 million in 1867 (aka, the best real estate deal ever—sorry, Manhattan).
- Became a U.S. territory, but was seen as too remote and too costly to develop.
- During WWII, Alaska became a key military base—proving its strategic importance.
- In 1959, it became the 49th state, partly to increase U.S. presence in the Arctic.

What Greenland Can Learn:
- A remote, icy land can still become a successful state.
- Military value can drive statehood—especially in the Arctic.

- People will mock you for being cold, but you can laugh all the way to the bank.

Hawaii's Journey to Statehood (1959)

- Annexed in 1898 after the overthrow of the Hawaiian monarchy.
- Became a U.S. territory, but was culturally distinct and geographically isolated.
- Played a crucial military role in WWII (Pearl Harbor).
- In 1959, became the 50th state, largely due to economic growth, military value, and political negotiations.

What Greenland Can Learn:
- Being culturally unique doesn't prevent statehood—Hawaii kept its identity.
- Strategic location can make Congress pay attention.
- Tourism + military bases = economic growth.

2. Comparing Greenland to Alaska and Hawaii

How does Greenland stack up against the two most recent states?

Category	Greenland	Alaska	Hawaii
Geography	Arctic, glaciers, fjords	Arctic tundra, mountains	Volcanic islands, beaches
Population	~56,000	~730,000	~1.4 million
Main Economy	Fishing, mining, tourism	Oil, fishing, tourism	Tourism, agriculture, military

Culture	Inuit traditions, Danish influence	Native Alaskan & Russian influences	Polynesian & Asian influences
Strategic Value	Arctic shipping routes, military bases	Arctic defense, oil reserves	Pacific military base, trade routes
Path to Statehood	Would require independence from Denmark or direct U.S. approval	Purchased from Russia, long transition	Annexed, became territory, military importance secured statehood

(Spoiler: Greenland makes Alaska look crowded and Hawaii look tropical... oh wait, Hawaii is tropical.)

3. What Worked in Alaska and Hawaii's Statehood Process?

What Worked Well?

* Strong Military Justification – Both states had major military importance (Alaska = Cold War security, Hawaii = Pacific stronghold).

* Economic Development Plans – The U.S. invested in infrastructure and industries to make both states financially viable.

* Federal Support & Integration – Statehood came with big federal investment in transportation, communication, and services.

Lesson for Greenland:
- If the U.S. sees Greenland as a critical defense asset, statehood becomes more realistic.
- A solid economic development plan would help ease the transition.
- Massive infrastructure investment is needed to make Greenland function as a U.S. state.

(Translation: If the Pentagon and Wall Street both want Greenland, Congress will probably listen.)

4. What Didn't Work Well?

* The "Too Remote" Argument Delayed Statehood
- Alaska was seen as too far, too cold, and too sparsely populated.
- Greenland faces an even bigger challenge—it's even smaller in population and farther away.

* Indigenous & Cultural Tensions
- Hawaii struggled with protecting Native Hawaiian culture under U.S. governance.
- Alaska's Indigenous communities had to fight for land rights and political representation.
- Greenland would need strong legal protections for Inuit traditions and land sovereignty.

Lesson for Greenland:
- The U.S. would need to ensure cultural protections for Greenland's Inuit population.
- Infrastructure, education, and representation would need serious investment.
- Greenland's remote location could slow down its transition—just like Alaska's did.

(In other words, it's going to take more than just "adding a star to the flag" to make Greenland statehood work.)

5. Applying These Lessons to Greenland

So, what's the best way forward for Greenland if it ever pursued U.S. statehood?

* Step 1: Strengthen Economic Ties First

Before jumping straight into statehood, Greenland and the U.S. could:

- Expand trade agreements for minerals, fish, and tourism.
- Increase American business investment in Greenland.
- Boost U.S. infrastructure aid to help Greenland modernize.

(Basically, date before getting married.)

* Step 2: Focus on Strategic Value

- If Greenland plays up its Arctic military importance, statehood becomes a national security issue rather than just an economic one.
- More U.S. military investment (bases, radar, Arctic research) could pave the way for a stronger U.S.-Greenland relationship.

(Because nothing makes Congress act faster than a military spending opportunity.)

* Step 3: Address Cultural & Political Autonomy

- Greenland must negotiate strong protections for its Inuit culture and language.
- It must ensure Indigenous governance structures remain intact.
- Representation in Congress must be fair and meaningful, not just symbolic.

(Because the last thing Greenlanders want is to be forgotten like Washington D.C. voters.)

Final Verdict: Can Greenland Follow the Alaska & Hawaii Model?

- Yes, if...
- It builds a stronger economy first.
- It plays up its military value to the U.S.
- It negotiates strong cultural protections before joining.

* No, if...
- It doesn't want to give up its autonomy.
- The U.S. doesn't commit to full infrastructure and economic support.
- The Greenlandic people oppose the idea altogether (which, currently, many do).

- Would statehood happen overnight? Nope—it took Alaska and Hawaii decades to gain statehood.

- Could Greenland become the 51st state eventually? Maybe—but only if the benefits outweigh the costs for Greenlanders.

(And only if America is ready for a state with more polar bears than people.)

CHAPTER

25

WHAT IF OTHER COUNTRIES FOLLOWED?

What If Other Countries Followed?
- Could this inspire similar statehood movements?
- Puerto Rico, Guam, and other territories
- Would the U.S. expand further?

So, Greenland has officially become the 51st state. The new star has been awkwardly crammed onto the American flag, presidential candidates are holding rallies in Nuuk, and someone in Congress has definitely suggested building a highway from Maine to Greenland (because why not?).

But now comes the bigger question:

- Could Greenland's statehood inspire other places to follow?
- Would Puerto Rico, Guam, or the U.S. Virgin Islands demand statehood next?

- And would America suddenly start "collecting" new states like Pokémon?

Let's explore how Greenland's decision could set off a domino effect—and whether this would mark the beginning of America's next big expansion.

1. Could Greenland's Statehood Inspire Similar Movements?

If Greenland can do it, why not us?

The moment Greenland joins the U.S., it will spark a national and global debate about other territories and regions that have been stuck in political limbo for decades.

Some places want statehood. Others don't, but might reconsider if Greenland prospers.

Let's look at the most likely candidates for U.S. statehood—or at least, closer integration.

2. Puerto Rico – The Most Obvious Next State?

If anyone has a right to feel left out when Greenland becomes a state, it's Puerto Rico.

Why Puerto Rico Might Demand Statehood

* It's been a U.S. territory since 1898 (that's 125 years—talk about a long engagement).
* Puerto Ricans are already U.S. citizens, but they can't vote in presidential elections.

* Statehood referendums have been held multiple times, and in the most recent one (2020), 52% voted in favor.

* It has a bigger population than 21 U.S. states (so the "too small" argument doesn't work).

Why Puerto Rico Hasn't Become a State Yet

* Congress keeps ignoring it – Mainly because of partisan politics (Republicans fear it would lean Democratic, and Democrats can't get enough votes to push it through).

* Some Puerto Ricans want full independence instead – A small but vocal movement exists.

* Would require massive economic restructuring – Puerto Rico has a different tax and legal system that would need to align with U.S. federal law.

Final Verdict:

- If Greenland becomes the 51st state, expect a loud, national debate about Puerto Rico finally becoming the 52nd.

- The phrase "If Greenland got statehood, why not us?" will be shouted on every news channel.

- Congress might finally be forced to make a decision rather than kicking the can down the road.

(Puerto Rico's reaction to Greenland jumping the line: "Oh, so NOW we're doing this?")

3. Guam, U.S. Virgin Islands, and American Samoa – The Forgotten Territories?

Most Americans forget that the U.S. still owns several territories around the world.

Would they also push for statehood after Greenland?

Guam – A Military Powerhouse

* Strategic military location in the Pacific (aka "The Unsinkable Aircraft Carrier").
* Already heavily integrated into the U.S. economy.
* Many residents support statehood—or at least full voting rights.

* Small population (~170,000 people).
* Could be too dependent on military funding to function as a full state.

(Would Guam want to be the 53rd state—or just settle for "statehood-lite"?)

U.S. Virgin Islands – America's Caribbean Paradise

* Would love the economic benefits of statehood.
* Already under U.S. laws and governance.

* Only ~87,000 people—too small for traditional statehood?
* Tourism-based economy could be vulnerable under full U.S. tax laws.

(Basically, if they become a state, they'd need a lot of financial support—aka, Uncle Sam's sugar daddy status.)

American Samoa – The Odd One Out

Fun fact: American Samoans are NOT automatically U.S. citizens—they're U.S. nationals. (Translation: They can live and work in the U.S., but they have to apply for citizenship.)

* Many would love full U.S. citizenship.
* Statehood could bring better economic support.

* Some want full independence instead.
* Statehood might disrupt traditional Samoan governance and customs.

(Would they go for it? Maybe... but they'd probably negotiate special conditions first.)

4. Would the U.S. Expand Even Further?

So... what if Greenland's statehood unleashed a new era of American expansion?

Would the U.S. suddenly start looking for more territories to "acquire"?

The Canadian Arctic – "Should We Join, Too?"

If Greenland thrives under U.S. statehood, what's stopping parts of Canada's Arctic territories from considering a similar move?

- Nunavut, Northwest Territories, and Yukon all face economic struggles and limited infrastructure.
- If Greenland gets federal funding, jobs, and better services, some Canadian Arctic communities might start wondering:

- Would we be better off as part of the U.S.?

(Canada's reaction: "Wait, what? No, stop it.")

The Falkland Islands – "Can We Join, Too?"

- The Falkland Islands are a British Overseas Territory in the South Atlantic.
- They have historical ties to the UK, but could see advantages in aligning with the U.S..
- If the U.K. ever wanted to offload some expensive overseas territories, could the U.S. offer them a deal?

(England: "We will never give up the Falklands!" America: "What if we throw in unlimited McDonald's?")

Cuba – The Wildest Possibility

Cuba has been politically distant from the U.S. for decades, but...

- If Cuba ever democratized, could a future government push for U.S. integration?
- Some Cubans in exile already support closer ties—though statehood would be extreme.

(Too crazy? Maybe. But if you told people in 1950 that Hawaii would become a state, they would've laughed, too.)

Final Verdict: Would Other Places Follow Greenland's Lead?

- Puerto Rico would immediately demand statehood.
- Guam and U.S. territories would push for more rights.

- Some Arctic and island territories might consider joining the U.S. for economic reasons.
- The U.S. would have to decide: Is this the start of a new era of expansion?

Would America suddenly start collecting states like Monopoly properties?

Probably not. But if Greenland prospers as the 51st state, don't be surprised if other places start thinking about their own futures under the Stars and Stripes.

(Because who doesn't love free federal funding and unlimited cheeseburgers?)

THE FUTURE OF THE ARCTIC
AND U.S. INFLUENCE

T he Future of the Arctic and U.S. Influence
- U.S. Arctic strategy and the impact of Greenlandic state-
hood
   - Climate change and Arctic policies
   - The role of Greenland in America's future

So, Greenland has officially joined the United States as the 51st state. The ink is dry, the polar bears are confused, and Congress is still arguing about whether to put a Starbucks in Nuuk first or a Taco Bell.

But beyond the politics and economic debates, there's a much bigger question:

   - What does Greenlandic statehood mean for the future of the Arctic?
   - How does it shape U.S. influence in the region?

- And will America's newest (and iciest) state become a key player in global affairs?

As climate change accelerates, new trade routes open, and geopolitical tensions rise, Greenland's role in America's Arctic strategy will only become more important.

Let's explore what Greenland's statehood means for U.S. influence, climate policy, and America's future in the Arctic.

1. The U.S. Arctic Strategy: Why Greenland Matters More Than Ever

Once upon a time, the Arctic was just a frozen, distant place where Santa lived and penguins (oops—wrong hemisphere) waddled around.

Now? It's a critical geopolitical battleground—and Greenland is sitting right at the center of it.

Why Does the Arctic Matter?

Strategic Location – Greenland gives the U.S. a prime position in the Arctic, allowing it to monitor Russian and Chinese activities.

New Trade Routes – As Arctic ice melts, new shipping lanes are opening up. The U.S. wants control over these lucrative routes to compete with Russia.

Natural Resources – The Arctic is rich in oil, gas, and rare earth minerals, and Greenland is a jackpot waiting to be tapped.

How Greenland Boosts U.S. Arctic Strategy

* More Military Presence – The U.S. can expand its Arctic bases in Greenland, strengthening NATO's northern defenses.
* Stronger Trade Control – America gets a bigger say in Arctic shipping regulations.
* More Research Opportunities – Greenland can become a hub for Arctic climate and energy research, funded by the U.S.

(Translation: Greenland might be cold, but its strategic value is on fire.)

2. Climate Change: The Arctic Is Melting—What Now?

Okay, let's address the elephant in the room (or rather, the polar bear on the iceberg).

Climate change is rapidly transforming the Arctic—and Greenland is one of the most affected places on Earth.

How does this impact Greenland's new role as a U.S. state?

Melting Ice = Rising Stakes

- Greenland's ice sheet is melting faster than ever, contributing to global sea level rise. ◈
- New fishing and trade routes are opening up, making Greenland's economic potential even bigger.
- America will have to balance economic interests with environmental responsibility (because drilling for oil in a melting Arctic might not be the best PR move).

Would the U.S. Protect Greenland's Environment?

* Potential for Renewable Energy – Greenland could be America's hub for Arctic wind and hydropower.

* Climate Research & Innovation – Statehood means more funding for Arctic environmental studies.

* But There's a Catch... – Some U.S. companies will definitely want to extract resources, which could clash with Greenland's sustainability goals.

Verdict: If Greenland joins the U.S., expect big debates over economic development vs. environmental protection.

(Spoiler: Congress arguing over this will be about as predictable as an iceberg breaking apart—slow at first, then a complete disaster all at once.)

3. The Role of Greenland in America's Future

With Greenland as part of the U.S., America's global position changes significantly.

More Control Over the Arctic

- The U.S. becomes a dominant Arctic power, directly challenging Russia's military expansion.
- Greenland provides a stronghold for NATO, securing key military and trade routes.

A New Economic Powerhouse?

- If developed properly, Greenland's fishing, tourism, and mining industries could become a major contributor to the U.S. economy.

- America gains more access to Arctic energy resources, reducing dependence on foreign oil and rare minerals from China.

A Key Player in Climate Diplomacy

- Greenland could become the face of America's Arctic environmental strategy, hosting global climate summits and research projects.
- The U.S. would be forced to take Arctic climate policies more seriously, with Greenland pushing for sustainable solutions.

(Translation: Greenland could be America's Arctic MVP—if Washington doesn't mess it up.)

4. Will America Handle Greenland's Statehood Well? (Or Will It Be a Mess?)

Let's be honest—the U.S. doesn't always handle new territories smoothly (cough Puerto Rico cough).

So, what are the challenges ahead?

The Big Questions

1. Will Greenland actually get fair representation in Congress?
(Or will it be treated like a political afterthought?)

2. Will the U.S. respect Greenlandic culture and autonomy?
(Or will it be forced into Americanization?)

3. Will the U.S. balance economic growth with environmental protection?
(Or will big corporations take over?)

Final Verdict:

- If managed well, Greenland could thrive as a U.S. state.
- If managed poorly, it could become America's "Arctic headache."

(Either way, it's going to be one wild political ride.)

Final Thoughts: Greenland's Role in the 21st Century

Greenland's statehood would be one of the biggest geopolitical shifts of modern times.

- It would solidify U.S. Arctic dominance.
- It would push America to take climate change seriously.
- It would reshape global trade and military strategy.

But the biggest question remains:

Would Greenland truly benefit from U.S. statehood, or would it be better off carving its own path?

That's the ultimate decision—and one that Greenlanders would have to make carefully.

(Meanwhile, the rest of the world will be watching—probably with popcorn.)

GREENLANDIC IDENTITY
AND INDIGENOUS

G reenlandic Identity and Indigenous Rights
· How would statehood affect Greenland's Indige-
nous Inuit population?
· U.S. history with Indigenous peoples vs. Greenland's
current autonomy
· Potential legal and social challenges in integrating
Greenland's unique identity
Rights

So, Greenland is now the 51st state of the United States. The
ink has dried, the new state flag is causing design debates, and
someone in Washington is trying to figure out how to pronounce
"Kalaallit Nunaat" without offending everyone.

But beneath the politics, the military strategies, and the economic arguments, there's a much deeper question:

- What happens to Greenland's Indigenous Inuit identity under U.S. statehood?

- Would Greenland maintain its unique culture, or would it face assimilation pressures?

- And, given America's complicated history with Indigenous rights, would this be a win or a warning sign for Greenlanders?

Statehood is more than just laws and economics—it's about people, heritage, and the future of a nation's identity.

Let's dive into how statehood could reshape Greenlandic culture, the legal and social challenges it would face, and what lessons the U.S. (hopefully) learned from its past with Indigenous peoples.

1. Greenland's Inuit Identity – What's at Stake?

First things first: Who are the people of Greenland?

Greenland is home to ~56,000 people, with about 90% identifying as Inuit—descendants of Indigenous Arctic peoples who have lived there for thousands of years.

Primary Language: Greenlandic (Kalaallisut), an Inuit language distinct from Danish and English.

Traditional Practices: Fishing, hunting (including seals, whales, and caribou), and a strong connection to the land.

Cultural Identity: Deep-rooted Inuit traditions, music, storytelling, and community-based governance.

Greenland isn't just a territory—it's a nation with a distinct identity.

So, the big question is:

Would becoming a U.S. state preserve that identity, or slowly erode it?

(Spoiler: It depends on how well Washington listens... and history tells us that's a mixed bag.)

2. U.S. History with Indigenous Peoples – A Cautionary Tale

The United States... does not exactly have the best track record when it comes to Indigenous rights.

(In fact, if history were a Yelp review, Native American communities would give the U.S. a solid 1-star rating with a "Would not recommend.")

Key Issues from U.S. History with Indigenous Peoples

* Forced Assimilation – Native American children were sent to boarding schools where they were punished for speaking their language or practicing their culture.
* Broken Treaties – The U.S. government signed hundreds of treaties with Native nations... then ignored or violated most of them.
* Land Seizures – Many Native lands were taken by force, fraud, or political maneuvering.
* Legal Struggles – Indigenous tribes had to fight for sovereignty, voting rights, and legal recognition—battles that continue to this day.

Lesson for Greenland: If history is any indication, Greenland would need serious legal protections to avoid these same patterns.

3. Would Greenland Keep Its Current Autonomy?

Before statehood, Greenland had a special political status under Denmark:

* Self-rule since 2009 – Greenland manages its own government, education, healthcare, and natural resources.
* Cultural Protections – Greenlandic is the official language, and Inuit traditions are integrated into governance.
* Denmark still handles defense and foreign policy, but Greenland has a say in key issues.

Under U.S. Statehood, What Would Change?

* What Greenland Could Keep:
- Greenlandic language protections, like Hawaii kept Hawaiian.
- State control over local education and cultural policies.
- Some autonomy in economic and land-use decisions.

* What Greenland Might Lose:
- Control over defense and foreign policy (now fully U.S.-controlled).
- Full economic independence (federal regulations and taxation would increase).
- Risk of Americanization – Would Greenlandic identity fade under pressure from English-language media, businesses, and politics?

(Imagine seeing the first McDonald's open in Nuuk—would it be exciting or a sign of cultural erosion?)

4. Legal Challenges: Can the U.S. Protect Greenlandic Identity?

For Greenland to thrive as a state while maintaining its culture, legal protections would be crucial.

What Greenland Would Need in a Statehood Agreement

* Recognition of Greenland's Inuit Government Structures – Can local leadership coexist with American state governance?
* Strong Indigenous Land Rights – Would Greenlanders keep control over hunting, fishing, and traditional land practices?
* Greenlandic as a Co-Official Language – Could it get the same status as Hawaiian in Hawaii?

(Or would Greenlandic slowly become a "heritage language" as younger generations shift to English?)

Could the U.S. Pass Special Protections for Greenland?

Maybe! Hawaii and Alaska set some precedents for Indigenous rights:

- Hawaii kept its Indigenous language officially recognized.
- Alaska has legal protections for Native Alaskan land claims and hunting rights.

Verdict: If Greenland negotiates a strong statehood deal, it could protect its Indigenous identity. If not, it risks losing autonomy over time.

(And if history is any guide, "trusting Washington" isn't exactly a strong plan.)

5. Social Challenges: Would Greenland Face Discrimination?

Let's talk social integration.

If Greenland joined the U.S., would Greenlanders be treated fairly?

Here's where things get tricky:

Historical Discrimination Against Indigenous Groups
- Native Americans and Native Alaskans have faced high rates of poverty, discrimination, and government neglect.
- Would Greenland's Inuit population face similar struggles under U.S. governance?

Media and Representation Issues
- Would Greenlandic voices be heard in national politics, or would they be treated as a political afterthought?
- How would U.S. media portray Greenland? As a serious cultural region or just "America's Coldest State"?

Verdict: If Greenland became a state, it would need strong social and political representation to ensure fair treatment.

(And also, the U.S. would need to learn how to correctly pronounce "Kalaallit Nunaat." Step one: Practice.)

6. Final Verdict: Would Greenlandic Identity Survive U.S. Statehood?

- It could survive—if Greenland fights for legal protections and autonomy.

- It could thrive—if the U.S. respects its unique culture and history.

* It could erode—if economic and cultural pressures lead to slow assimilation.

Would Greenlanders feel like full-fledged Americans, or would they feel like an overlooked Indigenous state on the edge of the map?

That's the biggest question—and the biggest challenge of all.

(Because no one wants to be "just another state"—especially not a place with 4,500 years of Indigenous history.)

Final Thoughts: What Would the People of Greenland Choose?

Ultimately, statehood is about more than just government policy—it's about preserving identity, culture, and self-determination.

- Would Greenlanders vote for statehood if they feared cultural erasure? Probably not.

- Could they negotiate a deal that preserves their autonomy? Maybe—but it would require serious legal guarantees.

Final Verdict: If Greenland wants to protect its Indigenous identity, it must approach statehood cautiously—or risk becoming just another chapter in America's complicated history with Indigenous peoples.

(And Greenlanders know better than to jump onto an iceberg without checking if it's melting first.)

TOURISM BOOM OR BUST?

Tourism Boom or Bust?
  ·   Would Greenland become the next Alaska or Hawaii for tourism?
  ·   The impact of increased American tourism on the environment and culture
  ·   How Greenland could capitalize on a potential tourism surge

So, Greenland is officially the 51st state of the United States. The American flag now has an awkwardly arranged 51 stars, someone is trying to open a Disney Ice Kingdom Resort, and travel agencies are offering Arctic vacation packages that include dog sled rides, iceberg selfies, and a Greenland-themed McFlurry.

But before Greenland turns into the next Alaska or Hawaii, we need to ask:

- Would statehood lead to a tourism boom—or a tourism disaster?

- Would Americans actually visit Greenland, or would they Google its weather and say, "Never mind"?

- And how could Greenland balance economic growth with protecting its pristine environment and unique culture?

Let's explore what happens when the world's largest island meets the world's most tourism-loving country.

1. Would Greenland Become the Next Alaska or Hawaii?

If Greenland became a U.S. state, it would instantly become a more accessible and attractive destination for American travelers.

Fewer travel restrictions.
Easier currency exchange (goodbye Danish krone, hello U.S. dollar).
Direct flights from major U.S. cities.

The biggest question is: Would Americans actually want to go?

Let's Compare: Greenland vs. Alaska vs. Hawaii

Feature	Greenland	Alaska	Hawaii
Climate	Cold. Always.	Cold, but with summer	Tropical paradise
Landscape	Icebergs, glaciers, fjords	Mountains, tundra, forests	Beaches, volcanoes, palm trees
Wildlife	Polar bears, whales, musk oxen	Bears, moose, bald eagles	Dolphins, sea turtles, tropical fish

| Tourism Appeal | Adventure & eco-tourism | Outdoor exploration | Beach vacations & luaus |

| Biggest Selling Point | See the Northern Lights & untouched Arctic landscapes | See Denali & grizzly bears | Surf, relax, eat pineapple on pizza |

Verdict:

- If you want to surf and drink piña coladas, go to Hawaii.
- If you want to hike and fish, go to Alaska.
- If you want to see the Northern Lights while standing on an iceberg, go to Greenland.

(Spoiler: Americans love adventure tourism. If marketed right, Greenland could absolutely be the next Alaska-style attraction.)

2. The Impact of Increased American Tourism on Greenland

Now, let's talk about the good, the bad, and the icy when it comes to a tourism boom.

* The Good: Economic Growth

Tourism would bring in jobs and money. Greenland could expect:
   More hotels, restaurants, and tour companies.
   More cruise ships stopping in Nuuk and Ilulissat.
   More outdoor adventure industries (dog sledding, snowmobiling, glacier hiking).

(Translation: Greenlanders could make money just by letting Americans ride sled dogs and take Instagram selfies with icebergs.)

* The Bad: Environmental Strain

Greenland is one of the most fragile ecosystems on Earth. More tourists could mean:

More cruise ships dumping pollution into Arctic waters.
More tourists trampling delicate tundra ecosystems.
More flights contributing to climate change (which is already melting Greenland's glaciers).

(Imagine tourists trying to pet a musk ox and accidentally causing a stampede. Not ideal.)

* The Cultural Impact: Could Tourism Erode Greenlandic Identity?

Greenland's culture is deeply tied to its Inuit traditions, language, and lifestyle. What happens if tourism over-commercializes it?

- Could traditional Inuit hunting and fishing practices be disrupted by conservation policies designed for tourists?
- Would Greenlandic culture be reduced to staged performances for American travelers?
- Would local towns become tourist traps instead of authentic communities?

(Hawaiians and Alaskans can relate—tourism brings money, but it also brings cultural challenges.)

3. How Greenland Could Capitalize on a Potential Tourism Surge

If Greenland plays its cards right, it can grow tourism sustainably without selling its soul.

Strategy 1: Eco-Tourism & Sustainable Travel

Instead of mass tourism, Greenland should focus on small-scale, high-value tourism.

* Limit cruise ship numbers to reduce environmental impact.
* Promote eco-lodges, sustainable hotels, and green travel options.
* Encourage responsible wildlife tourism—no feeding the polar bears.

(Think of it as tourism that doesn't ruin the very thing people came to see.)

Strategy 2: Cultural Preservation Through Tourism

* Offer authentic Inuit cultural experiences—not just tourist gimmicks.
* Support Greenlandic-owned businesses instead of big American chains.
* Teach tourists about Greenland's history and traditions rather than just treating it like an "Arctic Disneyland."

(Hawaii learned this lesson the hard way—better to control tourism before it controls you.)

Strategy 3: Winter Tourism & Northern Lights Adventures

Most people only think of traveling in summer. Greenland should flip the script and sell winter experiences like:

Northern Lights safaris.
Traditional Inuit sledding tours.
 Frozen waterfall climbing.
Hot springs with an Arctic view.

(Because who needs a beach when you can have a frozen wonderland?)

 Final Verdict: Boom or Bust?

- Greenland could become a major adventure tourism destination, like Alaska.
- If done sustainably, tourism could boost the economy without destroying the environment.
* If managed poorly, it could lead to cultural erosion and ecological damage.

- Would Americans visit Greenland? Yes—especially adventure seekers and eco-tourists.
- Would it turn into an overcrowded theme park? Probably not—unless someone actually tries to build a Disneyland on an iceberg.

(But let's be real: If Greenland had a Disneyland, Mickey Mouse would be wearing a parka.)

LANGUAGE AND EDUCATION

G reenlandic Language and Education Under U.S. Rule
·   Would English become the dominant language?
·   How education systems would change under U.S. poli-
cies
·   Preservation of Greenlandic and Danish languages

So, Greenland is officially the 51st state of the United States.

American businesses are setting up shop in Nuuk, Greenlanders are figuring out the correct pronunciation of "y'all," and
somewhere in Washington, a senator is suggesting replacing dog
sleds with electric snowmobiles to "modernize" transportation.

But now comes one of the biggest cultural questions of all:

- Would English replace Greenlandic as the dominant language?

- How would Greenland's education system change under U.S. policies?

- And could Greenlandic and Danish survive in an America where English is king?

Let's dive into the linguistic and educational shakeup that would come with Greenland's U.S. statehood—and whether the Inuit language and culture could stand the test of time.

1. Would English Become the Dominant Language in Greenland?

Right now, Greenland has a unique linguistic identity:

* Greenlandic (Kalaallisut) is the official language—spoken by over 90% of the population.
* Danish is widely used in administration, business, and international relations.
* English is spoken, but not fluently by most Greenlanders.

Key Question: Would Greenlandic survive under U.S. statehood, or would it fade away like many Indigenous languages in America?

How Have Other Non-English Languages Fared in U.S. States?

Hawaii (Hawaiian Language vs. English)
- Hawaiian was nearly extinct after decades of U.S. rule, but recent revival efforts have made it an official state language alongside English.
- Schools and businesses now promote Hawaiian, but English still dominates.

Alaska (Native Alaskan Languages vs. English)

- Alaska has 20+ Indigenous languages, but many have lost speakers due to English education policies.

- The Alaska Native Language Protection Act has helped preserve some, but English remains dominant.

Lesson for Greenland:

- If Greenland doesn't get strong legal protections for Greenlandic, it could follow the path of Native Alaskan languages—shrinking over time.

- If it fights for bilingual education, it could follow Hawaii's model, where the native language survives but doesn't dominate.

Would the U.S. Make English Mandatory in Greenland?

Likely Scenario: Greenlandic remains an official state language, but English becomes required for government, business, and education.

Worst-Case Scenario: Greenlandic slowly fades away as younger generations switch to English for jobs and social life.

Best-Case Scenario: Greenland implements strong bilingual policies like Quebec, keeping Greenlandic alive.

(Translation: If Greenland wants to keep its language, it needs to make a serious legal effort—because history shows English tends to take over.)

2. How Would Greenland's Education System Change?

Greenland's current education system follows a Scandinavian model, which is very different from the American system.

Current System (Danish Model):

* Free education from primary school to university.

* Focus on community-based learning and cultural preservation.

* Danish is required in schools alongside Greenlandic.

* No standardized testing obsession like in the U.S.

Now, let's throw in American education policies and see what happens.

Potential Changes Under U.S. Rule

School Curriculum Overhaul – Greenland's education system would likely shift to align with U.S. standards.

* Goodbye, Danish language requirements.

* Hello, American-style standardized tests and college entrance exams.

* U.S. history textbooks might not even mention Greenlandic history.

Would Greenland Schools Lose Their Cultural Identity?

Potential Risks:

- American school systems focus heavily on English and standardized testing, which could push Greenlandic culture and history to the sidelines.

- Greenlandic students might struggle in an English-dominant school environment if there's not a strong bilingual education policy.

- History classes would likely prioritize U.S. history over Greenlandic history.

(Because let's be honest, American schools barely teach Alaska's history—Greenland might not even get a footnote.)

How Greenland Could Preserve Its Education System

To avoid cultural erasure, Greenland would need to:

* Make Greenlandic a required subject in all schools (like Hawaii does with Hawaiian).
* Demand a unique curriculum that focuses on Greenlandic history, culture, and Indigenous rights.
* Maintain ties with Danish universities to keep Greenland's connection to Europe strong.
* Push for a dual-language system where Greenlandic and English are both official languages of education.

Verdict: Greenland could keep its educational identity—but it would have to fight for it in the U.S. legal system.

(Otherwise, a few decades from now, Greenlanders might only be able to say "hello" and "seal" in their own language.)

3. The Fate of Danish in Greenland – Would It Disappear?

One of the most overlooked consequences of Greenland joining the U.S. would be the decline of Danish influence.

Right now:
Danish is a required language in Greenland because of historical ties with Denmark.

Most higher education opportunities for Greenlanders are at Danish universities.

Many Greenlanders work in Denmark and have family there.

Now, imagine Greenland shifts from Denmark to the U.S.

Danish would no longer be required in schools.
Greenlanders might lose automatic access to Danish universities.
Danish-Greenlandic trade could decline as U.S. trade takes over.

Verdict: Danish might slowly fade out of Greenland, just like French faded out of Louisiana after it became part of the U.S.

(So, Denmark might need to start preparing for fewer Greenlanders applying to Danish universities and more applying to Harvard instead.)

Final Verdict: What Happens to Greenlandic Language & Education Under U.S. Rule?

- Greenlandic could survive—but only if legally protected.
- Danish would likely decline as Greenland integrates with America.
- Education would shift to a U.S. model, with potential cultural losses.
- Bilingualism could thrive—if Greenland fights for it.

Final Thoughts: Can Greenland Keep Its Identity?

Language is the heart of culture—and Greenlanders must decide:

Would they accept English dominance, or demand protections for their language?

Would they let U.S. education take over, or keep their own system alive?

Would they stay globally connected to Denmark and Europe, or fully integrate into the American education system?

Verdict: Greenland could balance statehood and cultural preservation—but it won't happen automatically.

(And let's be honest—if Greenlandic disappears, Americans will be very sad when they realize there's no English word for "a snowstorm so bad you don't bother going outside.")

GREENLAND AS AN ECONOMIC EXPERIMENT

G reenland as an Economic Experiment
- Could it become a tax haven or special economic zone?
- Lessons from Hong Kong, Singapore, and other economic hubs.
- How statehood could redefine Greenland's business landscape.

So, Greenland is officially the 51st state of the United States.

The first McDonald's in Nuuk has already opened, Wall Street investors are circling Greenland's rare earth minerals like hungry seagulls, and some genius in Congress has suggested renaming it "Greenerland" to attract more businesses.

But here's the real economic question:

- Could Greenland become a thriving economic powerhouse, like Hong Kong or Singapore?

- Would it be better off as a tax haven or a special economic zone?

- And how would statehood transform Greenland's business and financial landscape?

Let's dive into how Greenland could use its newfound American status to reinvent itself as an economic success story.

1. Could Greenland Become a Tax Haven or Special Economic Zone?

One of the most intriguing possibilities for Greenland under U.S. rule is that it could become a business-friendly financial hub—kind of like Singapore in the Arctic.

Low taxes? Check.
Attractive to global investors? Maybe.
Strategic location? Definitely.

What Is a Special Economic Zone (SEZ)?

A Special Economic Zone (SEZ) is a region where:
* Businesses get tax breaks and fewer regulations.
* Foreign investors are encouraged to set up shop.
* It becomes a hub for finance, trade, or technology.

(Translation: An SEZ is like putting a giant "OPEN FOR BUSINESS" sign on Greenland.)

Could Greenland Pull Off an SEZ?

- * Why It Could Work:
- Strategic Location: Greenland sits between North America and Europe—a perfect spot for an Arctic trade hub.
- Natural Resources: With access to rare earth minerals, fishing, and potential energy production, Greenland could become a resource-based SEZ.
- No Competition in the Arctic: Unlike Hong Kong or Dubai, Greenland would be the only major business hub in the far north.

* Why It Might Not Work:
- Small Population (~56,000 people)—who's running all these businesses?
- Infrastructure Problems—Greenland lacks roads, major ports, and strong internet connectivity.
- Harsh Climate—Tech billionaires love launching businesses in sunny tax havens, not on a glacier.

(Imagine Elon Musk trying to test self-driving cars in a blizzard. "Well, the car's lost under five feet of snow—call it a beta test!")

Verdict: If Greenland wants to be an SEZ, it needs massive investment in infrastructure and workforce development.

2. Lessons from Hong Kong, Singapore, and Other Economic Hubs

If Greenland wants to become a global business hub, it needs to learn from the world's most successful economic experiments.

Let's compare Greenland to three famous examples:

Hong Kong – The Ultimate Trade Hub

* Low taxes and business-friendly policies turned it into a financial powerhouse.
* Strategic location helped it become a major trade gateway.
* Massive foreign investment created a thriving business culture.

* Why This Model Is Hard for Greenland:
- Hong Kong has 7 million people—Greenland has 56,000.
- Hong Kong has a huge trade industry—Greenland mostly has fish and ice.

(Greenland's tourism slogan: "We don't have skyscrapers, but we have glaciers.")

Singapore – From Swamp to Superpower

* Smart government planning created a tech, trade, and finance hub.
* A small but highly skilled population helped it develop rapidly.
* Attracted global businesses with a stable legal and tax system.

* Why This Model Is Hard for Greenland:
- Singapore is hot and tropical—Greenland is cold and icy.
- Singapore has one of the best airport hubs in the world—Greenland has... um, small regional airports.

("Welcome to Greenland International Airport! Our only runway is currently frozen, please try again in the summer.")

Dubai – A Business Empire in the Desert

* Built an economic empire out of nowhere.
* Massive investment in tourism, real estate, and trade.
* Attracted billionaires and corporations with tax-free zones.

* Why This Model Is Hard for Greenland:
- Dubai has oil money—Greenland has fish and minerals, but no oil boom (yet).
- Dubai built mega-cities—Greenland has a population smaller than some U.S. college campuses.

(But imagine a giant ice hotel in Greenland called "The Arctic Atlantis." Now that would be something.)

Final Verdict: Greenland could learn from these economic models, but it needs to carve out its own Arctic niche.

3. How Statehood Could Redefine Greenland's Business Landscape

If Greenland became a state, what would actually change for businesses?

Potential Economic Benefits:
* More federal funding for infrastructure and business development.
* Easier access to U.S. trade networks.
* Potential to attract investment in Arctic shipping and energy.

Potential Economic Challenges:

* Would Greenland still control its resources, or would Washington take over?

* Would local businesses survive against major U.S. corporations?

* Would Greenland become dependent on U.S. subsidies instead of growing independently?

(Because let's be real—if Walmart and Starbucks show up in every town, it's a sign that things are about to change.)

3 Future Scenarios for Greenland's Economy

1. Greenland Becomes an Arctic Trade & Tech Hub
- Invests in technology, research, and Arctic-friendly industries.
- Becomes a hub for eco-tourism and Arctic commerce.
- Attracts global business leaders looking for a new frontier.

(Think of it as "Silicon Glacier" instead of Silicon Valley.)

2. Greenland Becomes America's Tax Haven
- Offers zero corporate tax rates to attract global businesses.
- Becomes a financial services hub for Arctic and European trade.
- Essentially becomes "the Switzerland of the Arctic."

("Greenland: Come for the tax breaks, stay for the Northern Lights.")

3. Greenland Stays Resource-Based
- Focuses on fishing, tourism, and mining, rather than tech or finance.

- Becomes a leader in Arctic resource extraction.
- Stays small, sustainable, and focused on preserving its way of life.

("We like our economy like we like our weather: Ice cold, but steady.")

Final Verdict: Could Greenland Become an Economic Powerhouse?

- It has the potential—but only with the right strategy.
- It needs massive investment in infrastructure and workforce development.
- It must balance economic growth with environmental and cultural preservation.

Would Greenland become the next Hong Kong, Singapore, or Dubai?

Maybe not—but it could still carve out its own niche as a unique Arctic economic hub.

(And at the very least, it could market itself as "The Coolest Place to Do Business." Literally.)

STATEHOOD AND AMERICAN
SOCIAL POLICIES

S tatehood and American Social Policies
- How would Greenland handle healthcare, social security, and welfare?

- Would Greenlanders benefit from U.S. entitlement programs?

- Comparing the U.S. and Nordic welfare models.

So, Greenland is officially the 51st state of the United States.

The American healthcare system has arrived, Social Security
offices are trying to figure out how to process payments north
of the Arctic Circle, and Greenlanders are wondering why people
keep talking about 401(k)s like they're a survival tool.

But this raises some big questions about how Greenland would
fit into America's social safety net:

- Would Greenlanders benefit from U.S. entitlement programs like Social Security and Medicare?
- How does the American welfare system compare to the Nordic model that Greenlanders are used to?
- And, most importantly, would Greenlanders have to deal with the same soul-crushing health insurance paperwork as the rest of America?

Let's dive into the social policy impact of Greenlandic statehood—and whether Greenlanders would be better off or stuck in bureaucratic limbo.

1. How Would Greenland Handle Healthcare?

First, let's talk about the biggest social policy difference between the U.S. and Greenland:

Healthcare. Greenland's Current Healthcare System (The Nordic Model)

As part of the Danish welfare system, Greenlanders currently enjoy:

* Universal healthcare—paid for by the government.
* Free medical treatment, including hospital care, prescriptions, and specialist visits.
* No private insurance system—everything is covered through taxes.
* Medical flights for remote areas are government-funded.

Translation: Greenlanders never have to worry about going bankrupt from a hospital visit—they just show up, get treated, and leave (without a bill that looks like a phone number).

What Happens Under U.S. Statehood? (The American Model)

Now, Greenland joins the U.S.—where healthcare is... let's say, complicated.

Here's what would change:

* No more free universal healthcare.
* Greenlanders would have to get private health insurance or qualify for Medicaid/Medicare.
* Hospital bills would now include a mystery fee labeled "facility charge" that costs more than a snowmobile.

(Imagine a Greenlander seeing a $20,000 ER bill for the first time: "Wait... you have to PAY for an ambulance ride?")

Would Greenlanders Qualify for Medicare & Medicaid?

* Yes, if they meet income or age requirements.
* Medicare would cover seniors, and Medicaid would help lower-income residents.
* But it wouldn't be as seamless as their current universal system.

Verdict: Greenlanders would technically get U.S. healthcare benefits, but they would lose their current universal coverage in exchange for a more complicated system.

(And let's be honest—no one in Greenland is excited about dealing with U.S. insurance companies.)

2. Would Greenlanders Benefit from U.S. Entitlement Programs?

Now, let's talk about social security, unemployment benefits, and welfare programs.

Social Security & Retirement

Right now, Greenlanders receive Danish pension benefits, which are:

* Guaranteed and stable (funded by high taxes).
* Enough to live comfortably in retirement.
* Not dependent on the stock market or 401(k)s.

Under U.S. statehood:

* Greenlanders would switch to Social Security, which depends on how much you earned in your lifetime.
* Greenlanders would need to contribute to Social Security taxes for years before qualifying.
* If they worked long enough, they'd get Social Security payments—but they might be lower than what Denmark currently provides.

(So, Greenlanders would go from "guaranteed pension" to "hope the system doesn't collapse before you retire.")

Unemployment Benefits

Right now, Greenland's unemployment system follows the Nordic model, meaning:

* If you lose your job, the government supports you.
* Benefits last longer and provide a livable wage.
* Job training programs help people find new work.

Under U.S. statehood:

* Unemployment benefits are time-limited and vary by state.
* There's no universal job placement program like in Denmark.
* However, some U.S. job training programs exist to help people reenter the workforce.

(Translation: "Good luck finding a job, but we'll give you some unemployment benefits for a while before cutting you off.")

Welfare & Social Assistance

* Greenlanders would qualify for U.S. welfare programs like food stamps (SNAP) and housing assistance.
* The U.S. has more programs for lower-income families, including child tax credits.
* But the programs vary wildly by state and can be hard to access.

Verdict:
- Greenlanders would technically have access to welfare, but it wouldn't be as reliable as the current Nordic model.
- Statehood could bring more U.S. federal funding for social programs—but it wouldn't replace the benefits they currently get from Denmark.

(So, in short: More paperwork, more eligibility hoops, fewer guaranteed benefits.)

3. Comparing the U.S. and Nordic Welfare Models

Let's stack these two systems side by side to see what Greenland would gain and lose under U.S. statehood.

Category	Greenland (Nordic Model)	U.S. Statehood Model
Healthcare	Universal, free at point of use	Private insurance, Medicare, Medicaid
Retirement	State-funded pensions	Social Security (based on lifetime earnings)
Unemployment	Long-term benefits, job training	Time-limited, varies by state
Welfare	Strong social safety net	Varies by state, eligibility requirements
Education	Free university tuition	Student loans, limited free tuition programs

Final Verdict:

- Greenlanders would gain access to U.S. welfare programs, but they would lose the simplicity and security of the Nordic model.
- Health and retirement benefits would become more complex and less generous.
- Greenlanders might have to navigate American bureaucracy for the first time—and they probably won't love it.

(Imagine a Greenlander filling out their first U.S. healthcare form: "Why are there 17 different plans, and why does none of them cover dental?")

Final Thoughts: Would Greenlanders Be Better Off Socially?

- They would gain access to American welfare programs, but with more restrictions.

- They would get U.S. Social Security, but it might be worse than their current pension.

* They would lose universal healthcare and enter America's complicated system.

Would Greenlanders appreciate American social policies?

Probably not.

The Nordic model is deeply ingrained in Greenlandic society, and switching to the U.S. system would be a huge adjustment—one that many Greenlanders might not be willing to make.

(Because when you've had free healthcare and secure pensions your whole life, "work harder and hope for the best" isn't exactly a selling point.)

GREENLAND'S RELATIONSHIP WITH CANADA

G reenland's Relationship with Canada
- Would Canada be an ally or competitor in the Arctic?
- Shared Indigenous heritage and cultural ties.
- Potential cooperation or conflicts between Greenland and Canada.

So, Greenland is now the 51st state of the United States.

The American flag has been awkwardly adjusted to include 51 stars, Greenlanders are learning what a "Super Bowl" is, and Canada is eyeing the whole situation like a neighbor watching a loud new family move in next door.

Which raises the question...

- Would Canada be an ally or a competitor in the Arctic?

- How would Greenland's shared Indigenous heritage shape its relationship with Canada?

- Would the U.S. and Canada become Arctic BFFs—or is this the beginning of an icy rivalry?

Let's break down what happens when Greenland goes American—and how Canada reacts.

1. Would Canada Be an Ally or Competitor in the Arctic?

First, let's address the giant frozen elephant in the room:

The Arctic is becoming one of the most important geopolitical battlegrounds of the 21st century.

It's home to:

* Vast natural resources (oil, gas, and rare earth minerals).

* New shipping routes opening due to melting ice.

* Competing claims from the U.S., Canada, Russia, and other Arctic nations.

Before Greenland Became a U.S. State

Canada and Greenland had a friendly relationship, both as part of the Arctic Council and as neighbors in the North Atlantic. They cooperated on:

- Environmental protection.

- Indigenous rights and cultural preservation.

- Fishing and resource management.

After Greenland Becomes U.S. Territory?

Now, things get a little more complicated.

Canada and the U.S. are allies, but they don't always agree on Arctic issues.

Greenland's new U.S. status could shift the balance of Arctic power.

Canadian leaders might worry that U.S. expansionism is creeping closer.

(Imagine Canada saying, "First you bought Alaska... now Greenland? What's next, Nunavut?")

Verdict: Canada would still be a close partner, but it might start seeing Greenland as a competitor in Arctic trade, resource extraction, and military presence.

2. Shared Indigenous Heritage and Cultural Ties

Now, let's shift gears and talk about what Greenland and Canada have in common—specifically, Indigenous heritage.

Both Greenland and Northern Canada are home to Inuit communities, who have lived in the Arctic for thousands of years.

Similarities Between Greenlandic and Canadian Inuit Culture

* Traditional Inuit hunting, fishing, and survival skills.
* Shared language roots—Greenlandic and Inuktitut are closely related.
* Strong cultural traditions, storytelling, and community-based governance.
* Both regions rely on sled dogs (because Arctic traffic jams are just snowdrifts).

(Fun fact: The Inuit Circumpolar Council represents Inuit communities across Greenland, Canada, Alaska, and Russia—so these groups have always stayed connected.)

Would U.S. Statehood Affect These Cultural Ties?

If Greenland becomes part of the U.S.:

* Could Indigenous rights policies diverge? Greenland would now fall under U.S. federal law, while Canada follows a different legal system for Indigenous rights.
* Would Canada's Inuit feel pressure to align more with Greenland—or vice versa?
* Could there be more cooperation on cross-border Indigenous policies?

Verdict: Greenland and Canada's Inuit communities would still have strong cultural connections, but their political and legal frameworks might start to drift apart.

(And the real question: Would Canada's Inuit start asking, "Hey, can we get those U.S. federal benefits too?")

3. Potential Cooperation or Conflicts Between Greenland and Canada

Scenario 1: Arctic Cooperation – The Best Case Scenario
If Greenland and Canada play nice, they could:

Work together on Arctic environmental protection.
Develop shared Arctic shipping routes.
Expand cultural and academic exchanges between Inuit communities.

Boost Arctic research and climate change initiatives.

(Imagine Greenland and Canada co-hosting an annual "Arctic Summit" where the dress code is parkas and the main topic is "How to Keep Your Toes from Freezing.")

Scenario 2: Arctic Competition – The Frosty Rivalry Scenario
But... what if they don't play nice?

Canada and Greenland (now U.S. territory) could compete for Arctic shipping dominance.
Greenland might attract more investment, stealing business from Canada's Arctic ports.
Resource conflicts could arise if mining and drilling rights overlap.

(Imagine Canada saying, "We called dibs on that Arctic trade route first!" and the U.S. saying, "Finders, keepers.")

Scenario 3: Canada Gets Jealous – The "What About Us?" Scenario
Let's not forget:

Canada has its own remote, underdeveloped Arctic territories.
If Greenland gets massive U.S. investment, Canada's Arctic regions might say:
- "Hey, what about us?"

Could Canada's Arctic territories demand better treatment from Ottawa?
Would some Canadian Arctic communities even joke about switching to U.S. control?

("If Greenland gets free infrastructure from Washington, why do we still have dirt roads up here?" – Some guy in Nunavut, probably.)

Verdict: Canada might feel pressure to invest more in its Arctic regions if Greenland starts booming under U.S. statehood.

(Translation: If Greenland gets new roads, airports, and internet, Canada might have to step up its game in the Arctic, too.)

Final Verdict: Would Greenland and Canada Stay Friendly?

- Yes, they'd still be allies—but with new tensions over Arctic power.
- Yes, their Indigenous communities would remain culturally close.
- But economic and territorial competition could cause some friction.

Would Canada fully embrace Greenland's U.S. statehood?

Probably not. Would Canada secretly hope the U.S. doesn't start eyeing more Arctic land?

Absolutely. (Because let's be honest, Canada already deals with enough "U.S. expansion" every time a Tim Hortons gets replaced by a Starbucks.)

CONSPIRACY THEORIES AND GREENLAND

Conspiracy Theories and Greenland
- Would statehood fuel wild theories?
- Hidden U.S. military bases, UFOs, and secret Arctic projects.
- How Greenland could become the next Area 51.

So, Greenland is now the 51st state of the United States.

The first Walmart has opened in Nuuk, government officials are holding meetings about polar bear safety, and somewhere in a dark corner of the internet, conspiracy theorists are having a field day.

Because let's be real—any time the U.S. expands, the internet fills with wild theories faster than you can say, "The truth is out there."

- Would statehood fuel a wave of Greenland-based conspiracy theories?

- Are there already secret U.S. military bases hiding under the ice?

- Could Greenland become the next Area 51—but colder?

Let's dive into the frozen depths of conspiracy speculation and see why Greenland might soon have more tinfoil hats than tourists.

1. Would Statehood Fuel Wild Conspiracy Theories?

The moment Greenland officially becomes a U.S. state, the internet will explode with theories about what's really going on up there.

Theory 1: "The U.S. Is Hiding Something Under the Ice"
Reality: Greenland is melting due to climate change.
Conspiracy: "The ice isn't melting—it's being THAWED to reveal a hidden civilization!"

Theory 2: "The U.S. Bought Greenland for Alien Technology"
Reality: The U.S. sees Greenland as strategically important.
Conspiracy: "Greenland isn't a military asset—it's covering up an alien crash site!"

(Because, obviously, if UFOs crashed anywhere, it would be the least populated, most frozen place on Earth.)

Theory 3: "Greenland Will Be the Next Global Surveillance Hub"
Reality: Greenland is great for radar and satellite tracking.

Conspiracy: "Greenland is where they'll build the next big NSA spy center!"

(Translation: Snowden 2.0 might need a parka.)

Verdict:
- Statehood would 100% fuel new conspiracy theories.
- Greenland's remote location makes it the perfect setting for secretive government projects.
- People already believe wild things about Antarctica—Greenland would be next!

(It's only a matter of time before someone on YouTube says, "The ice is just a cover for an underground city.")

2. Hidden U.S. Military Bases, UFOs, and Secret Arctic Projects

The real fuel for these theories? The fact that the U.S. already has military secrets in Greenland.

The Real-Life Secret: Camp Century (The 1960s "Ice Base")

In the 1960s, the U.S. built Camp Century, a nuclear-powered research facility under Greenland's ice.

It was supposed to be for scientific research, but... surprise! It was actually part of Project Iceworm—a secret plan to hide nuclear missiles under the Arctic.

Spoiler: The ice was less stable than expected, and the project was abandoned.

(Translation: The U.S. was already trying to build a James Bond villain lair in Greenland—so of course, people assume they're still up to something.)

UFO Sightings in the Arctic

Greenland's vast, empty sky = perfect place for "UFO" sightings.
Any unidentified military tests = instant alien conspiracy.
Thule Air Base has been linked to UFO rumors for years.

(Because nothing screams "extraterrestrial hotspot" like a frozen wasteland with almost no people to witness anything.)

Could Greenland Become the Next Area 51?

Let's compare:

Category	Area 51 (Nevada)	Greenland (Future Area 51.5?)
UFO Theories?	* Yes	* Yes (coming soon)
Military Secrets?	* Yes	* Probably
Remote Location?	* Yes (desert)	* Yes (icy wasteland)
Easier to hide stuff?	* No (too many tourists)	* Yes (almost nobody lives there)
Likelihood of TikTokers sneaking in?	* High	* Low (too cold)

Verdict:
- Greenland is PERFECT for a new "secret base" theory.
- The fact that most Americans will never visit makes it even more mysterious.

- If the government actually WAS hiding something, this would be the place.

(Translation: If the U.S. wanted to create a new mystery to distract people, Greenland would be the perfect setting.)

3. How Greenland Could Capitalize on the Conspiracy Buzz

If Greenland is destined to be the next hub of wild theories, they might as well make some money off it.

Ideas for Greenland's "Secret" Tourism Industry:

* "Top-Secret" Thule Air Base Tours – Come see where the U.S. isn't hiding aliens!
* "UFO Landing Spot" Arctic Tours – Visit the frozen tundra where "something crashed" (allegedly).
* "Camp Century Escape Room" – Can you survive the real Cold War experiment?
* Greenland's Own "Storm Area 51" Event – Except, instead of running through a desert, you're sledding through the Arctic.

(Because let's be real, conspiracy tourism is BIG business—just ask Roswell, New Mexico.)

Final Verdict: Is Greenland the Next Great Conspiracy Hotspot?

- Yes, if statehood brings new U.S. military expansion.
- Yes, if old Cold War secrets get declassified.
- Yes, because the internet LOVES wild theories about frozen places.

Would Greenland ever actually replace Area 51?

Maybe not—but it's going to get a lot more attention from people who think the government is up to something.

(And let's be honest, the moment someone sees an "unidentified flying object" over Greenland, the internet will officially lose its mind.)

GREENLAND AND
CRYPTOCURRENCY

G reenland and Cryptocurrency
- Could Greenland become a crypto hub?

- The potential for blockchain-based governance.

- U.S. financial laws and their impact on Greenland's economic future.

So, Greenland is now the 51st state of the United States.

The first Starbucks has opened in Nuuk, Washington is debating how many federal highways Greenland really needs, and somewhere in Silicon Valley, tech billionaires are eyeing Greenland's cold climate for the next big thing in cryptocurrency.

Which brings us to the big digital question:

- Could Greenland become the world's next crypto hub?
- Would blockchain technology work in Arctic governance?

- How would U.S. financial laws affect Greenland's economic future?

Let's dive into how Bitcoin, Ethereum, and Dogecoin (because let's be honest, people would try) could find a new home in the Arctic.

1. Could Greenland Become a Crypto Hub?

Cryptocurrency miners and blockchain investors LOVE cold climates for one simple reason:

Bitcoin mining = a lot of computer heat.
Greenland = natural air conditioning.

Why Crypto Miners Would Flock to Greenland

* Cold temperatures = cheaper cooling costs for mining operations.
* Massive amounts of hydroelectric power = sustainable energy for crypto farms.
* Low population = plenty of space to set up massive server farms.

(Imagine a Bitcoin server farm the size of a glacier, except this time, the ice won't melt from climate change—it'll melt from overheating GPUs.)

But let's get realistic—could Greenland actually become the crypto capital of the Arctic?

What Other Crypto Hubs Teach Us

Iceland: Already a hotspot for Bitcoin mining due to cheap renewable energy and cold climate.

El Salvador: Made Bitcoin legal tender, but the experiment has been... rocky.

Singapore: A global crypto hub thanks to friendly regulations and tech innovation.

Would Greenland follow one of these models?

Verdict:

- Yes, it could attract miners—but it would need to create crypto-friendly policies.

- Yes, it could use blockchain for economic innovation—but only if the U.S. allows it.

- No, it wouldn't become the "next El Salvador"—because let's be real, Greenlanders don't want to be an economic experiment.

2. The Potential for Blockchain-Based Governance

Now, let's get futuristic. What if Greenland embraced blockchain—not just for finance, but for governance?

Could Greenland Use Blockchain for Public Services?

* Digital IDs & Voting Systems: Secure elections without voter fraud.

* Smart Contracts for Fishing Licenses: Automate Greenland's biggest industry.

* Transparent Government Budgets: Track every krone (or now, every dollar?) on the blockchain.

(Imagine if every taxpayer dollar in Greenland was traceable on a public ledger—Congress would probably panic at the thought!)

Would Blockchain Governance Actually Work?

Pros:
- Corruption-proof record-keeping.
- Instant transaction verification.
- No need for massive government bureaucracy.

Cons:
* Requires fast, widespread internet (Greenland doesn't have that yet).
* Cybersecurity risks—what happens if hackers steal all the fish quotas?
* The U.S. government might not approve of "too much" transparency.

Verdict: Blockchain-based governance is possible, but Greenland would need massive infrastructure upgrades first.

(Translation: We need to get them better WiFi before we start talking about decentralized government.)

3. U.S. Financial Laws and Their Impact on Greenland's Economic Future

Now for the least fun part of the crypto discussion—regulations.

Before statehood: Greenland had looser financial laws under Denmark, meaning it could experiment more with digital finance.

After statehood: Greenland would fall under strict U.S. financial laws, including:

* The SEC (Securities and Exchange Commission) = More oversight of crypto markets.

* Anti-Money Laundering Laws = No sketchy offshore crypto havens allowed.

* Higher Federal Taxes = Crypto profits would now be taxable by the IRS.

(Imagine Greenlanders opening their first IRS tax notice: "Wait... we have to report our Bitcoin gains?!")

Would the U.S. Allow Greenland to Be a Crypto Hub?

If Washington sees crypto as a "threat" to financial stability, expect heavy restrictions.

* If the U.S. sees Greenland as an Arctic "Silicon Valley," it might encourage innovation.

(Translation: It depends on whether Congress understands crypto... which, given history, isn't looking good.)

Verdict:

- Greenland could attract crypto businesses—but only within U.S. legal limits.

- Blockchain governance is an option—but not without major tech investments.

- U.S. financial laws could slow down Greenland's crypto dreams before they even start.

(And let's be honest—if the U.S. can barely regulate Wall Street, they're not letting Greenland go full "Bitcoin Nation" anytime soon.)

Final Verdict: Could Greenland Become the Crypto Capital of the Arctic?

- Yes, it has the right climate and energy potential.
- Yes, blockchain could improve governance—if it gets the right infrastructure.
* No, the U.S. would regulate it heavily.
* No, Greenlanders probably don't want their entire economy based on digital coins.

Would Greenland be the next big crypto hub?

Probably not—but it could use blockchain to modernize its economy if it plays by U.S. financial rules.

(And let's be honest, even if Greenland doesn't embrace crypto, someone will try launching "ArcticCoin" just for fun.)

THE FINAL VOTE – COULD THIS ACTUALLY HAPPEN?

The Final Vote – Could This Actually Happen?
- Realistic timeline for statehood
- Political and economic considerations
- Closing thoughts on feasibility

So, after 34 chapters of Arctic deep dives, political ice-breaking, economic speculation, and more dad jokes than Greenland has sled dogs, we've finally arrived at the ultimate question:

- Could Greenland actually become the 51st state of the United States?
- How long would it take?
- Would it ever get enough political and economic support?

Let's take a realistic look at what it would take for Greenland to officially trade Danish rule for the Stars and Stripes—and whether this whole idea is genius or just geopolitical fantasy.

1. What Would the Timeline for Greenlandic Statehood Look Like?

Becoming a U.S. state is NOT fast or easy.

It takes years—sometimes decades—of legal, political, and economic negotiations before a new state can join the Union.

Let's look at how long it took for past territories to become states:

State	Became U.S. Territory	Became a State	Time It Took
Louisiana	1803 (purchased from France)	1812	9 years
Texas	1836 (independent republic)	1845	9 years
Alaska	1867 (purchased from Russia)	1959	92 years
Hawaii	1898 (annexed by U.S.)	1959	61 years
Puerto Rico	1898 (territory)	Still waiting...	126+ years

(Translation: Greenland should pack a lunch. This could take a while.)

Step 1: Greenland Votes for Independence from Denmark

Before Greenland can join the U.S., it has to become fully independent from Denmark.

Right now, Denmark still controls:
* Defense and foreign policy
* Some financial aid to Greenland

For Greenland to even consider U.S. statehood, it would first need a national referendum to break away from Denmark.

Would Greenland vote for independence?

Maybe... but not right away.

Greenlanders value self-rule, but they also rely on Danish economic support.

If Greenland became independent, it would lose Denmark's financial assistance, meaning it would need major U.S. investment to survive.

(Translation: Greenland would have to decide between "freedom with financial uncertainty" or "sticking with Denmark and keeping things stable.")

Step 2: The U.S. Congress Approves Greenland's Statehood

Once Greenland is independent, the U.S. Congress has to approve statehood.

* A simple majority in both the House and Senate is required.
* Greenland would also have to draft a state constitution.

The biggest political hurdle? Partisan politics.

Would Republicans support adding a new state?

Would Democrats push for Greenland if Puerto Rico still isn't a state?

Would Denmark get really, REALLY mad?

(Spoiler: Denmark would definitely be salty.)

Realistic Timeline for Greenland's Statehood

- 2035-2040 – Greenland holds an independence vote (assuming they want to leave Denmark).
- 2040-2050 – U.S. and Greenland negotiate terms of statehood.
- 2050-2060 – Congress debates and eventually approves Greenland as a U.S. state.

Verdict: The earliest Greenland could become a state is mid-to-late 21st century.

(Translation: Your grandkids might live in a world where Greenland is a U.S. state—but you probably won't.)

2. Political and Economic Considerations

Would Washington Support Greenland's Statehood?

Pros:
- Increased U.S. Arctic influence (take that, Russia and China!).
- New military positioning in the Arctic.
- Access to rare earth minerals and shipping routes.

* Cons:
- Expensive investment in infrastructure and social programs.
- Potential conflicts with Denmark and NATO.
- Very small population = minimal political influence.

(Would Congress really fight for a state with fewer people than Wyoming?)

Would Greenland's Economy Survive Statehood?

Right now, Greenland relies on:
* Fishing (biggest industry)
* Danish financial support
* Tourism and mining (slowly growing)

Under U.S. statehood, Greenland would need:
Massive infrastructure upgrades
More investment in sustainable industries
Strong legal protections for Greenlandic culture and land rights

(Translation: Greenland would need billions in federal funding before it could function as a U.S. state.)

Verdict: Greenland could eventually become self-sustaining—but it would take decades of U.S. investment.

3. Closing Thoughts on Feasibility – Could This Actually Happen?

After 35 chapters, what's the final answer?

- Yes, it is theoretically possible for Greenland to become a U.S. state.
- Yes, there are strategic and economic reasons for the U.S. to want Greenland.
- Yes, Greenlanders might consider it—IF the benefits outweigh the costs.

* But no, it's not happening anytime soon.

* No, Denmark wouldn't just give up Greenland without a fight.

* No, Congress isn't eager to add a new state that isn't Puerto Rico first.

The Final Verdict: Should Greenland Become the 51st State?

Would the U.S. say yes?

- Maybe... but not without serious debate and investment.

Would Greenland vote for it?

- Not right now—but maybe in the future, if independence became more viable.

Would Denmark let it happen?

- Not without a diplomatic battle.

Final Thoughts: Is This Idea Wild Speculation or a Real Possibility?

On one hand:

- It sounds like geopolitical science fiction ("The United States of Greenland" just feels weird).

On the other hand:

- The U.S. has a history of expanding in unexpected ways (Louisiana Purchase, Alaska, Hawaii).

Final Conclusion: Greenland becoming the 51st state is un-likely—but not impossible.

(So, if you ever see a U.S. Senator casually bringing up Green-land in a speech, keep an eye on your map—things could get in-teresting.)

And That's a Wrap!

Thank you for joining this humorous yet serious exploration of whether Greenland could become America's next state.

Would it happen? Probably not.
Would it be fascinating to watch? Absolutely.
Would the first Starbucks in Nuuk get a line around the block? Guaranteed.

Until then, stay warm, stay curious, and remember: Greenland might be cold, but its geopolitical future is heating up.

THE END... OR IS IT?

CONCLUSION

The Greenlandic Dream – A Reality or Just a Fun Idea?
- Summarizing key arguments
- Encouraging readers to think critically about statehood
- Final humorous reflections on Greenland and America

And so, dear reader, we have reached the end of our epic Arctic journey—a 35-chapter odyssey through history, politics, economics, tourism, military strategy, cryptocurrency, and even UFO conspiracies.

We've cracked jokes, dug into serious geopolitical questions, and explored every reason why Greenland could (or couldn't) become the 51st state.

But now it's time for the final verdict:

- Is Greenlandic statehood a serious possibility—or just a fun "what if" scenario?
- Would Greenlanders ever say yes?
- And most importantly... would Greenland really want to deal with American reality TV?

Let's wrap it all up, highlight key takeaways, and end on one last, ice-cold note.

1. Summarizing Key Arguments: The Case For and Against Statehood

Before we pack up our snowshoes and go home, let's quickly recap what we've learned.

* The Case FOR Greenland Becoming the 51st State

- Strategic U.S. Expansion: A Greenlandic state would give America stronger military positioning in the Arctic—a big win against Russia and China.

- Economic Potential: With the right investment, Greenland could become a hub for fishing, tourism, rare earth mining, and Arctic trade.

- Stronger Infrastructure & Social Services: Greenlanders could gain access to better healthcare, education, and development funds—assuming Washington is willing to pay up.

- Americans Would Love It: Northern Lights tourism, dog sledding, and ice hotels? Sounds like the next big thing for adventure-seeking travelers.

(Imagine the first Greenland-themed amusement park—"Disneyland Nuuk," where the log flume ride is just... well, actual melting ice.)

* The Case AGAINST Greenland Becoming the 51st State

* Greenlanders Probably Don't Want It: Right now, Greenland is closer to seeking full independence from Denmark than joining the U.S.—they want self-rule, not new rulers.

* Would Washington Even Approve It? The U.S. hasn't added a new state in over 60 years—and Congress can't even agree on lunch, let alone a new state.

* Expensive, Remote, and Logistically Tough: Greenland has fewer than 60,000 people but would need billions in infrastructure investments to function as a U.S. state.

* Cultural Differences: Greenland has a deeply Inuit-based society with Nordic influences—would they really want to swap Danish pastries for deep-fried Oreos and chili cheese fries?

(Let's be honest—if Greenlanders ever had to watch the Super Bowl with its bizarre commercials, they'd have some questions.)

2. Encouraging Readers to Think Critically About Statehood

But beyond the humor, this book asks an important question about statehood, expansion, and self-determination:

Who gets to decide when a country or region joins another nation?

Should powerful countries keep expanding, or focus on their existing territories?

Can small, remote regions like Greenland thrive on their own, or do they need a bigger ally?

At its core, Greenland's future isn't just about geopolitics—it's about identity, self-governance, and the right to choose one's destiny.

(Because at the end of the day, no one wants to be forced into a relationship they didn't ask for—just ask Texas about its complicated history with Mexico.)

3. Final Humorous Reflections on Greenland and America

After everything we've explored, one thing is certain:

Greenland might not become the 51st state anytime soon, but it will continue to play a fascinating role in global politics.

And hey, if nothing else, Greenland can always milk its new-found fame for all it's worth:

* Tourism Slogan Idea: "Visit Greenland—Before America Buys It!"
* Reality Show Idea: Arctic Housewives of Nuuk—drama, ice fishing, and more drama.
* T-Shirt Idea: "Make Greenland Green Again" (which would be a bold move considering all the ice).

(And let's be real—if any U.S. president ever actually made a serious offer to buy Greenland again, Denmark's response would be a polite but firm, "Nej.")

Final Verdict: The Greenlandic Dream – A Reality or Just a Fun Idea?

So, could Greenland become the 51st state?

Yes, in theory—there's a legal path, and the U.S. has a history of expanding.

No, in practice—Greenlanders don't want it, and it would take decades to happen.

Maybe, if political and economic realities shift in unexpected ways.

But for now...

Greenland remains Greenland.

Denmark remains Denmark.

And America? Well, America will probably move on to the next big debate—like whether to finally add Puerto Rico as a state first.

(Or, you know, whether pineapple belongs on pizza—but that's a geopolitical debate for another book.)

Final Thought: What If Greenland Did Become a U.S. State?

Would America be better off?

Would Greenland regret it?

Would Greenlanders start wearing cowboy hats ironically?

Who knows.

But one thing's for sure—it would make one heck of a trivia question.

And if this book has taught you anything, it's this:

* The world is full of wild political possibilities.
* Sometimes, the best ideas sound crazy at first.

* And even if Greenland never joins the U.S., at least we had a fun time thinking about it.

So, until next time—stay curious, stay skeptical, and remember:

The world is an ever-changing place... and sometimes, the most unexpected ideas turn out to be true.

APPENDICES

Appendices

Appendix A: Key Facts About Greenland

General Information
- Official Name: Kalaallit Nunaat (Greenland)
- Political Status: Autonomous territory within the Kingdom of Denmark
- Capital: Nuuk
- Population: ~56,000 (One of the least populated places on Earth)
- Area: 2.16 million square kilometers (~836,000 square miles)
- Official Language: Greenlandic (Kalaallisut)
- Currency: Danish Krone (DKK)
- Primary Industries: Fishing, mining, tourism, Arctic research

Appendix B: The Process of Becoming a U.S. State

1. Independence from Denmark
- Greenland would first need to vote for independence in a national referendum.
- Denmark would have to recognize Greenland's independence and settle financial and political transitions.

2. Petitioning for U.S. Statehood
- Greenland would need to formally apply for statehood.
- The U.S. Congress would have to approve the request by a simple majority vote in both the House and Senate.
- Greenland would need to draft a state constitution and integrate into U.S. governance systems.

3. Full Statehood Process
- Congress passes an enabling act outlining Greenland's transition into statehood.
- A final statehood referendum would be held in Greenland.
- Once all agreements are completed, Greenland officially joins as the 51st state.

(Estimated Timeline: 20-50 years, depending on political and economic conditions.)

Appendix C: Other U.S. Statehood Candidates

Besides Greenland, there are several territories and regions that have debated U.S. statehood:

Region	Current Status	Statehood Likelihood
Puerto Rico	U.S. Territory	High (frequent referendums)
Washington, D.C.	U.S. Capital District	Medium (political challenges)
Guam	U.S. Territory	Low (more support for autonomy)
American Samoa	U.S. Territory	Low (cultural and legal issues)

| U.S. Virgin Islands | U.S. Territory | Low (small population, economic concerns) |

(Translation: Greenland wouldn't be the only place in line for statehood—it would have competition.)

Appendix D: Fun Facts About Greenland

- Despite its name, Greenland is mostly ice—about 80% of it is covered by a massive ice sheet.
- The U.S. already has a military base in Greenland! Thule Air Base has been operating since 1951.
- Greenland is home to the world's fastest-moving glacier, Jakobshavn Glacier, which moves over 30 meters (~98 feet) per day.
- There are no roads connecting Greenland's towns. Travel is done by boat, plane, or, if you're adventurous, dog sled.
- The Greenland Shark is one of the longest-living vertebrates, with some estimated to be over 400 years old!
- Greenland was "discovered" multiple times—by Vikings, European explorers, and eventually, American politicians with checkbooks.

Appendix E: The Greenland Statehood Debate – Pros and Cons

Pros of Greenland Joining the U.S.
* Stronger Infrastructure: U.S. investment would improve roads, airports, and internet access.

* Economic Growth: More access to American markets, business opportunities, and funding.

* Military and Strategic Benefits: The U.S. could solidify Arctic defense against Russia and China.

* Social Services & Healthcare: Greenlanders could receive U.S. federal benefits like Social Security and Medicare.

Cons of Greenland Joining the U.S.

* Loss of Autonomy: Greenlanders might have less control over their government and resources.

* Cultural Erosion: Risk of Greenlandic language and traditions being overshadowed by American influence.

* Complex Bureaucratic Transition: Navigating U.S. laws, taxes, and regulations would be a challenge.

* Potential Danish Backlash: Denmark might strongly oppose Greenland leaving its kingdom.

Appendix F: What If the U.S. Bought Greenland Instead?

If statehood seems unlikely, what about an outright U.S. purchase of Greenland?

Historical Precedents

- 1803: The U.S. bought Louisiana from France for $15 million.

- 1867: The U.S. bought Alaska from Russia for $7.2 million.

- 1946: The U.S. actually offered Denmark $100 million for Greenland—Denmark said no.

Modern Price Tag?

Economists estimate Greenland's "value" at anywhere from $1 trillion to $10 trillion, depending on:
- Its resource potential (rare earth minerals, oil, fishing).
- Strategic military positioning.
- The economic value of Arctic shipping lanes.

(Translation: If America ever tried to buy Greenland again, it wouldn't be cheap.)

Appendix G: Hypothetical U.S. Flag with Greenland as the 51st State

One of the biggest logistical problems? Where do we put that extra star on the American flag?

Design Options
A new 51-star pattern (awkward, but possible).
A return to a 13-stripe star cluster (like the original colonies).
Just add one big Greenland-shaped star somewhere in the corner.

(If Greenland does become a state, let's hope the flag designers are good at geometry.)

Appendix H: Pop Culture and Greenlandic Statehood

Movies That Could Be Made If Greenland Became a State
"51st State: The Coldest Addition" – A political thriller about the dramatic road to statehood.

"Arctic Independence" – A Greenlandic version of Independence Day, but with polar bears instead of aliens.

"Frozen 3: Greenland Joins the U.S." – Elsa lobbies Congress for statehood.

Songs That Could Be Written

"God Bless Greenland" – A new verse for "God Bless America."

"Sweet Home Nuukabama" – A rock anthem for Greenland's U.S. integration.

(Because what's a new state without its own theme song?)

Final Note: What Happens Next?

So, what should we expect in the next 50-100 years?

* Greenland will continue gaining more autonomy from Denmark.

* The U.S. will likely expand its military and economic interests in Greenland.

* Statehood will remain an interesting, but unlikely, possibility.

But who knows? The world is full of surprises.

Maybe one day, we'll all be toasting with Greenlandic coffee at the first Fourth of July parade in Nuuk.

Or maybe, just maybe...

Greenland will stay exactly as it is—independent, icy, and watching from a distance as the U.S. continues its chaotic political reality show.

THE GREENLAND STATEHOOD ACT

The Greenland Statehood Act

With this bill, Greenland would be legally, politically, and economically integrated into the United States while maintaining
its cultural identity and Arctic heritage. However, the road to
statehood would be complex and require careful negotiation with
Greenland, Denmark, and international stakeholders.

If this bill were ever introduced in Congress, expect heated debates, international reactions, and plenty of skeptical Greenlanders wondering if this is all just another wild American idea.

(And yes, expect memes about the U.S. trying to "buy" Greenland all over again.)

Could it happen? Maybe. Would it be complicated? Absolutely.
But one thing's for sure—it would be one of the most fascinating
geopolitical events of the 21st century.

Here's a draft of a U.S. Statehood Bill for Greenland, outlining
the process by which Greenland would be incorporated into the
United States as the 51st state.

The Greenland Statehood Act of [Draft]

A Bill to Provide for the Admission of Greenland into the United States of America as the 51st State

Section 1: Short Title

This Act may be cited as the "Greenland Statehood Act of [Year]."

Section 2: Findings and Purpose

(a) Findings

Congress finds that:

1. The people of Greenland, through a democratic referendum, have expressed their desire to join the United States as a state.

2. Greenland has a distinct cultural, economic, and geopolitical significance to the Arctic and the United States.

3. Greenland has been a self-governing entity within the Kingdom of Denmark, with increasing autonomy in political and economic affairs.

4. Greenland's strategic location enhances U.S. national security and economic interests, including military positioning, natural resource development, and Arctic trade.

5. The United States recognizes and respects the cultural heritage, Indigenous rights, and economic needs of Greenlanders.

(b) Purpose

The purpose of this Act is to:

1. Provide a legal framework for the admission of Greenland as a state of the United States.

2. Establish the rights and responsibilities of the State of Greenland.

3. Facilitate a smooth transition of governance, infrastructure, and federal integration.

Section 3: Admission of Greenland as a State

Upon fulfillment of the requirements set forth in this Act, Greenland is hereby declared to be admitted into the United States of America on an equal footing with all other states in all respects.

Section 4: Transition to Statehood

(a) State Constitution

1. Greenland shall draft and adopt a state constitution, consistent with the U.S. Constitution and federal law.

2. The proposed constitution shall be submitted to the people of Greenland for approval in a referendum.

3. The constitution shall ensure the protection of Indigenous rights, the preservation of Greenlandic culture, and environmental sustainability.

(b) Temporary Governance

1. A Greenland Transition Commission (GTC) shall be established to oversee the transition, consisting of representatives from Greenland, the U.S. Congress, the Department of State, and the Department of the Interior.

2. The GTC shall operate for a period of up to five (5) years to facilitate Greenland's full transition into the United States.

(c) Representation in Congress

1. Greenland shall elect two Senators to the U.S. Senate.

2. Greenland shall elect one Representative to the U.S. House of Representatives, subject to reapportionment based on census data.

Section 5: Legal and Economic Integration

(a) U.S. Citizenship

1. All citizens of Greenland shall become U.S. citizens upon statehood.

2. U.S. citizenship shall not preclude the recognition of Greenlandic Indigenous identity and cultural autonomy.

(b) Taxation and Economic Transition

1. Greenland shall be subject to federal taxation but may receive an economic transition period of up to ten (10) years with modified tax rates to ensure economic stability.

2. The federal government shall provide economic assistance for infrastructure development, education, and healthcare improvements.

3. A joint U.S.-Greenland Economic Development Authority shall be established to manage investment projects, energy resources, and sustainable economic growth.

(c) Federal Oversight and Jurisdiction

1. The laws of the United States shall apply to Greenland upon statehood, except as provided for in this Act.

2. The judicial system shall be integrated into the federal court system, with an initial transition period where Greenlandic courts handle certain local matters.

Section 6: Protection of Indigenous Rights and Cultural Heritage

(a) Language and Cultural Protection

1. Greenlandic (Kalaallisut) shall be recognized as an official state language alongside English.

2. Federal and state agencies operating in Greenland shall provide services in Greenlandic and English.

3. Greenland shall have the authority to preserve, protect, and promote Indigenous culture, education, and traditions.

(b) Indigenous Land and Resource Management

1. Greenland's Indigenous communities shall retain collective rights over traditional lands and waters.

2. Natural resource development shall be subject to environmental sustainability guidelines and local approval.

Section 7: Military and National Security

(a) U.S. Military Presence

1. Thule Air Base and other U.S. military installations shall continue operations under U.S. Department of Defense authority.

2. Greenland shall have input in decisions related to military expansion and Arctic security policy.

(b) Arctic Security and Defense Strategy

1. The U.S. shall establish a Greenland Arctic Security and Defense Council to coordinate policies between Greenland and the U.S. military.

Section 8: Environmental Protections and Climate Change Policies

(a) Arctic Preservation Initiatives

1. The U.S. shall recognize Greenland's unique Arctic environment and implement policies to protect its ecosystems.

2. The U.S. shall allocate federal funds for climate change mitigation, sustainable energy projects, and scientific research in Greenland.

(b) Renewable Energy Development

1. Greenland shall receive priority funding for hydroelectric, wind, and sustainable energy projects.

2. A special Green Energy Fund shall be created to support the transition away from fossil fuels.

Section 9: Implementation and Timeline

1. Referendum: Within 12 months of this Act's passage, the people of Greenland shall hold a binding statehood referendum to accept or reject statehood.

2. Transition Period: A transition period of up to 10 years shall be implemented to fully integrate Greenland's legal, economic, and political systems into the United States.

3. Statehood Effective Date: Upon successful completion of the transition process, Greenland shall be officially declared the 51st state of the United States.

Section 10: Severability Clause

If any provision of this Act is found to be unconstitutional or invalid, the remainder of the Act shall remain in effect.

Section 11: Enactment

This Act shall take effect immediately upon passage by both Houses of Congress and signature by the President of the United States.